Face Your Fears

by Jared Munson

To purchase additional copies of this book, contact the publisher:
Herald Publishing House
P.O. Box 390
Independence, MO 64051-0390 USA
Phone: 1-800-767-8181 (toll-free) or (816) 521-3015
Canada: 1-800-373-8382 (toll-free)
Web site: *www.HeraldHouse.org*

For more information on Community of Christ contact:
Missionary Office
Community of Christ World Headquarters
1001 West Walnut
Independence, MO 64050-3562
1-800-825-2806 or (816) 833-1000; extension 2242

To contact the Chattanooga Urban Ministries Team:
Chattanooga Urban Mission
2428 North Chamberlain Avenue
Chattanooga, TN 37406-3815

© 2005 Herald Publishing House
Independence, Missouri

Book design by Matt Mills

All rights reserved. Published 2005
Printed in the United States of America

10 09 08 07 06 05   5 4 3 2 1

ISBN-10 0-8309-1153-7
ISBN-13 978-0-8309-1153-0

In memory of my great friend,
Matt Wilhoite

Contents

Preface	07
01: Baseball Bats and Jesus	11
02: Love Your Neighbor	23
03: Pillows versus Guns	35
04: White Chocolate	47
05: Popcorn in a Drug House	57
06: Mental Illness in Algebra Class	65
07: Jesus and My Middle Finger	75
08: Messin' with Shootist	89
09: An Issue of Blood	99
10: Miracle of the Prayer Ball	113
11: Fear in the House	123
12: Maggie at the Midnight Movies	131

Preface

As I wrote in my first book, *Courageous Witness: A Teenager Shares Jesus*, my parents have always prayed that the core gift of my life would be courage. Courage is never about the lack of fear. Courage is about being willing to do the hard work necessary to face your fears.

As I write this preface to my second book, I am a high school senior with some fears knocking on the door of my heart. I will soon be leaving my home congregation where I have served as a co-pastor for the last four years and facing the fear of having to start living out my witness in a new faith environment. I will soon be leaving my home and parents to go to college and face the fear of not having my parents at my fingertips for their advice and wisdom. I will soon be heading to college to gain a bachelor's degree yet fearing that my learning disability and poor study habits may keep this from happening. I am becoming a young adult and facing the fear of growing up and slowly being forced to put my youthfulness behind me. Most young adults seem to find themselves on the outside of their church community, and I fear that this could happen to me.

What I am trying to say is the call to be brave is not going to go away for me or for those of you reading this book. We must find the courage to face our fears and rise above them always. Yes, I have many fears to face, but I hope the courage of the Jesus of my youth will grow and become the courage of the Jesus of my young adult life.

Before going any further, I want to say thank you to those who read my first book and to the Community of Christ. It is an honor to be a member of this courageous movement. It is a honor to be called out by Jesus to live out my witness in this movement. Thank you to all who support me in my journey.

My parents are very generous people. I see courage in their generoristy. It is not easy to give your heart, time, love, money, and precious witness away. Yet my parents have been courageous in being so generous in risking all they have, know, and process for the sake of winning lost souls to Jesus.

In trying to follow the examples of my mentors, each week I write an experience of my life to remind me of the call to be brave and generous with my heart. It takes courage to share my private and personal experiences with others. Yet I want to be generous with the true life stories in which I have seen the witness of Jesus' love make a tremendous difference in people I've known personally.

I also want to share my witness of the requirement of courage in living out a Christian witness. Courage and invitation are required of every Christian whether they are senior citizens, adults, young adults, teenagers, youth, or children. We must seek to be brave enough to discover the joy of being generous with our invitations to others to come and follow Jesus.

My parents have tried to teach me to be brave and generous. I have failed many times at both. My dad has told me more times than I can remember that because he loves me so much, it is his desire that I find the joy of generous invitation. My dad and mom are so generous in their invitations for others to find Jesus and his living gospel of hope.

All too often, people appear to be selfish with their relationship with Jesus and want to keep it private and personal. Well, I think Jesus wants us to be a brave people—brave enough to be generous with our invitation and witness, to share our personal stories of Jesus with others and risk being laughed at, misunderstood, and rejected.

My purpose for writing this second book is because I again feel led to do so. But it is also my hope that those who read it may somehow, by the mysterious touch of the real Jesus, find the courage to be generous with their invitations to others. We must become bold inviters for Jesus.

I am only eighteen and yet I know that the number-one obstacle for Christians to sharing our faith and personal stories of Jesus is *fear:* the fear of *failing;* of *being rejected;* of *losing the respect* of our friends, co-workers, and loved ones; of *offending* the very people we want to help; of *driving people away* from Jesus because of our lack of knowledge, preparation, and training. It is safer for us to remain silent and withhold our witness and our invitation.

My friends, it is safer for me to remain silent, also. When I share the experiences of my faith journey in book form, I open myself to criticism, misunderstanding, and misjudgment. Since my first book, some people have gotten the impression that I am a so-called "Goody Two-Shoes." I am not. I am my father's son and will leave it at that. Some people think I am a smart guy who finds writing and reading easy, but I have made the honor roll only once in my life. I read when I have to. I do write, but it has always been for my own enjoyment; believe me, no one can make sense of much of it. Some people think I am a confident snob. It takes much prayer and hard work for me just to find the confidence to get out of bed each day.

I share this with you because I want you to know that writing another book is requiring me to have courage. Yet I seek to be generous with my invitation. I write this book to invite you to become generous with your invitation and witness. We must be generous with our talents, time, energy, knowledge, money, love, and witness of invitation.

I have survived my youth—of being the son of a hard-living and focused church planter—because of the love of Jesus Christ. Jesus has been my friend and my personal Savior for as long as I can remember. It's not because I deserve it or earn it. Jesus is alive to me because others in my young life were brave enough to be generous with their invitation for me to come and allow Jesus into my personal life. I chose to respond to their invitations and I have been generously blessed to have a relationship with Jesus. I am a sinner yet Jesus generously remains in my life. I am also a coward yet Jesus still generously remains in my life. I am a failure *yet Jesus generously remains in my life.*

Because Jesus continues to generously stay in my life, I have been able to be a witness and invite others into a life journey with him. This makes me feel that I am a very wealthy young person. It is my hope in writing this second book that Jesus will touch your life in a way that helps you find the courage to be generous with your invitations to invite others to church, to the waters of baptism, and to a lifelong commitment of serving Jesus Christ. Thank you for caring enough to read my book. I hope you enjoy it.

If you do enjoy it, please invite others to read it also. Let us live the message of the good news of Jesus through our courageous and generous invitations. Be courageous. Be generous.

— *Jared Munson*

01
Baseball Bats and Jesus

Many Americans have memories of playing Little League baseball. We dream about making that unbelievable catch, scoring the winning run, hitting the winning RBI, throwing out the runner at home plate, and the list goes on. I have all those common memories of baseball, but I also have a unique memory about it that has helped shape my faith journey.

I was six years old and just a few months earlier had moved from Illinois to the South. I moved because my dad accepted a position as a church planter and missionary. I already was missing my grandparents, aunts, uncles, and cousins, whom our move required us to leave behind. But it was summertime and things were looking up. I was signed up for summer league baseball. My focus was turning from the family members I had left behind to the joy of playing baseball.

I was going to practices, making new friends on my team, and feeling great about playing. Naturally, I had dreams of being the next Babe Ruth. Playing baseball was going to be awesome. I was so proud of my uniform. I loved the fact that every day Dad would find time to play baseball with me in the backyard. I was living the dream of practically every six-year-old American boy.

Reflections

- Where were you living when you were six years old? Who was living with you in your household?
- How old were you the first time you can remember moving? Why did you move?
- What was your favorite sport or group activity during your early elementary years? How do you feel about this same activity now?

More of the Story:

My baseball dreams quickly turned into nightmares. This change didn't come about because of my athletic abilities or any sport injuries. It came about because some of my teammates' parents disapproved of my church affiliation.

After my first game, our team went out for pizza. The parents began talking and getting to know each other. Because my family had only lived there a few months, we were the least known. Therefore, all the parents wanted to know what my parents did for a living and why we had moved to the area.

These inquiries are usually harmless, but not for me with my stupid Munson luck. My dad's response resulted in my first personal memory of being rejected. He said he was a minister and that God had called us to the area to plant a new church. Everyone seemed happy with this until they asked what church my dad worked for. When Dad told them the name of the church, people suddenly quit talking to us. We all noticed this change in attitude immediately.

Due to the name of our church at the time and years of public misinformation and misunderstanding, those parents concluded that my family was not Christian. Not only did they believe we were not Christians, they believed we were evil and that I was a bad kid.

The very next night, some of those parents came to our house with a minister from another church. They informed my parents that they could not "legally" kick me off the baseball team, but they wanted to make it clear that my participation on the team was unwanted. They said we were devil worshipers and a religious cult. They asked my parents to take me off the team.

As I sat there listening to this, I just kept thinking how much I loved Jesus. In my off-key voice, I kept singing softly, "Jesus

Loves Me." It was the hope in my little six-year-old wisdom that if they heard me singing that song, they would understand how wrong they were. I mean, we had a big picture of Jesus hanging on the wall in our living room that I knew they saw; surely it was evidence of whom we worship. We also had a big family Bible on our stereo in that same room. Even our church's name at the time had "Jesus Christ" in it. But nothing seemed to convince them that I loved Jesus.

After a long and heated discussion, the visitors left our home. I saw anger in my dad's face and tears in my mom's eyes. I felt it was entirely my fault that my parents were hurting and that I had done something wrong by playing baseball. I ran to my room and cried. I kept praying over and over, telling Jesus that I *did* love him and so did my mom and dad.

Reflections

- Have you ever been rejected by someone or some group because of what they thought you believed about God? If so, how has that rejection affected your witnessing spirit?
- Have you ever rejected someone or some group because of what you think they believe? If so, how can you repent of this?
- What would you do about this situation if your child were being pressured off the team because of your church affiliation?
- What would you do if you were the coach of this team?
- What is your reaction to the "Christian" parents who came making the request? Do you feel most Christians are judgmental of others? Why or why not? How does this affect Christianity as a whole?

More of the Story:

My dad spent the rest of the night on the phone talking to people about our visitors. I do not know who he called or what was said. My mom came to my room and talked with me. We talked about our feelings from all this junk.

I just could not understand why people thought badly of us and why Jesus did not help us with this situation. My mom and I prayed together several times that night. I remember her telling me that in the New Testament of the Bible some people thought Jesus was evil and that they even finally caused him to be killed. She told me that Jesus said if we were going to be his real disciples, we would have to face rejection and some of the same things he faced. Well, that was fine and good for his disciples, but I was just a little boy who wanted to play baseball.

Finally my dad came to my room. We talked for a little while and then he asked me to do something that I did not understand. He asked me to pray for the people who came to our house and wanted to kick me off the team. He also told me that I had to be nice in my prayer.

Well, I will tell you the truth. I wanted to pray and ask Jesus to breathe fire down on those folks or make them super ugly. But Dad taught me that night for the first time about our Christian call to be peacemakers. He read to me from the Bible that we are called to pray for and love our enemies. This was the first time in my life that I prayed for people I did not like. I must also confess that this has not been the only time that I was called to pray for people I did not like. Praying may be hard, but believe me, it is really hard when you have to pray for people you just don't like. There have been a lot of people in my young life whom I did not like and therefore I have spent a lot of time in this type of prayer.

Please do not get the impression that I do not get mad or into fights. I might sometimes know what the right thing is to do, like turning the other cheek, but that does not mean I always choose to do it. But I guess if doing the right thing were easy, we would not all be sinners.

After our prayer time, Dad told me that it was too late for me to join another baseball team or another league. He told me that my coach was sorry about the incident and he still wanted me to stay on the team. We then talked about several options we could take. My parents were responsible for making some of those choices, but they gave me the responsibility of deciding whether or not I wanted to quit the team.

As an only child, I have been spoiled in many ways. But my parents have caused me to make some tough decisions on my own all my life. This was one of those times. I did not have any older siblings to discuss the matter with. I had no friends or any relatives close by. I did not even have a pastor or a youth director—just my parents. My parents had done a great job of laying out the options and the possible outcome of each option. The problem was I did not like any of the choices.

Baseball was supposed to be fun. I was just a little boy who wanted to pretend to be Babe Ruth. I wanted to have baseball stories like my cousins and my dad. But it sure did not seem to be any fun at the moment. It sucked.

Reflections

- What would you choose if you were Jared? Would you quit the team? Give up on baseball? Stay on the team?
- Have you ever truly prayed for your enemy or for someone you did not like? If so, did the prayers help?

- Do you believe that in our Christian calling to be peacemakers we should pray for our enemies? Does praying for our enemies show weakness or courage? Do you think bringing peace may sometimes require us to physically fight?

The Rest of the Story:

I decided to stay on the team and learn how to play baseball so good that everyone would want me on his or her team. It was going to require work and probably some more tears, but nobody was going to make me *not* play baseball. My parents supported me in my decision, and so my baseball career continued.

But this incident did not go away just because I decided to stay on the team. My decision to stay on the team resulted in me sitting the bench a lot during the next few games. It also meant that my

teammates did not say anything to me except to cuss me. It also meant that before a game or practice when my teammates were playing pitch and catch, that I would have to just throw the ball in the air and catch it. I called this playing pitch and catch with the angels. I would throw the ball up and they would throw it down to me. I know it sounds stupid, but it gave this six-year-old boy the ability to survive.

One day after practice, the parents were having a team meeting. My dad was gone out of town somewhere to offer ministry. My mom was sitting in the meeting by herself and was being ignored. My teammates took this opportunity to let me know that I was not wanted on the team.

About seven or eight of them surrounded me with ball bats and I was told to "quit the team or die." I picked up my ball bat and prepared myself for a butt whipping. I was scared and all alone. I was praying, my heart was pounding, and I was so scared that I was probably crying. I was silently asking Jesus to rescue me. Jesus was going to answer my prayer for help in a way that I would never forget.

One of my teammates ran into the circle and held up his bat. He told the other boys that if they wanted to fight me they were going to have to fight him, too. He said, "I may not go to church, but I know that God is about helping people, not beating people up. You are all wrong. Jared is my friend."

If you ever thought that one person couldn't make a difference then you have never been facing a butt kicking alone. My teammate joining me in battle made a tremendous difference in my life. I felt courage in that moment. Right then and there I learned the power that lies in one person. My teammate standing by my side gave me confidence that we would survive no matter how many kids with ball bats attacked us. Jesus sent me help through the courage of another six-year-old teammate.

Now being that I mentioned peacemaking earlier, you all are probably expecting a peaceful solution to this story. Well, no such luck. This ain't television! It's real life! My hero and I got beat up. We both had bloody noses and lips. I even got hit in the head with a bat. (Maybe I can use that head injury as an excuse for my low GPA.) Praise God that the adults broke up the fight or we probably would have ended up with broken bones. This was my first so-called gang fight and it was a painful experience. I am not sure that I even landed a punch on anyone. Believe me, we got hammered.

Well, this also ended the rejection situation. When my dad got home, he paid a personal visit to the homes of all the boys who ganged up on us that day. I am not sure if it was the Spirit of God, threats of lawsuits, or some of my dad's street justice that ended the situation. But from the day of the fight on, no one else has ever tried to kick me off a team.

I went on to play organized baseball for the next six years. I won the MVP award a couple of times and made the All-Star team each year. However, my love for baseball got lost. I am not sure if the incidents written about here played a role in that or not. I just know that one day I decided that I didn't want to play any more baseball and began to focus more on basketball.

Since this story occurred, our church has voted to change its name to Community of Christ. I am proud of our name change for many reasons. One is that it now gives us the chance to tell people who we really are. I believe our new name could have saved me from a butt kicking, but then I never would have experienced the power that comes when one person is willing to stand with us.

The boy who stood by my side is still my friend today. He gave me a valuable lesson of how much stronger someone is able to be when they know they are not standing alone. He, too, has given up baseball. He even attends cell church with me often. I have not gotten him baptized yet, but he taught me a life-long lesson about the strength and difference one person can make.

Final Reflections

- What are your reflections on this story? What emotions, if any, did it stir up in you?
- Has anyone ever come to your aid when you were facing something alone? Have you ever stood beside someone when they were facing danger?
- Did you see any courageous moments in this story?
- How can we help change religious judging?

What I've Learned

This experience taught me several things. It taught me how much of a difference just one person can make. My nameless friend in the story made a difference because he got involved. Because of him, I know firsthand how important it is to be involved in hard situations. We have to stand up for others when the odds are against them even if it means we place ourselves in danger and face being unpopular. After all, didn't Jesus hang on the cross and suffer pain for us? Being willing to suffer for others is never fun but sometimes it is necessary.

I've learned that many Christian denominations are going through name changes. It seems strange to me that we live in a country that was partly founded on freedom of religion yet we are still so quick to force people into being outcasts and even abused because of their church or religion. Is it really freedom of religion when we want a little boy off our baseball team because we fear the name of his church and what we think his religion teaches? To me freedom of religion means people have the right to believe whatever they want and that we will stand strongly by their side to support this right even if we totally disagree with their beliefs. Freedom of religion is for those who disagree with us as well as for those who agree. I love Jesus but I also support the right of others not to love him. I will do all I can to try to convince people how great life is with Jesus Christ as personal savior and friend. I will also do all I can to defend the right of someone to choose not to listen to my stories if that is their choice.

I've learned that Christians have enough challenges and battles to face without fighting one another. I also learned that passing judgment on others because of their religion or because of what we think we know about their beliefs is very wrong.

It takes more courage to love and pray for enemies than it does to fight them. Forgiving is a hard thing to do but it is worthwhile. It takes more strength and guts to be a witness for peacemaking than it does to face a 100-mph fastball from a wild pitcher.

02
Love Your Neighbor

Love your neighbor. These three words guided me through a time of decision making when I was a little boy. These three words came to my heart and childlike mind one night as I lay in bed seeking out what was the right thing for me to do. No, I am not saying that some supernatural voice spoke to me with a heavenly message. My young life has had enough natural drama and challenges without those types of experiences being added to my journey. These three words came to me when I was eight years old in a calm and reassuring way. How they came is unimportant. The important thing is they came and gave me guidance.

When my family moved to Chattanooga to respond to Jesus' call to plant a church, it meant we came without knowing anyone. When I started to school, the school required the name of someone locally they could call in case my parents would be unavailable during an emergency. My parents chose two ladies from my neighborhood to be my contacts for school.

The decision was cool with me. These two women raised great big dogs and were into sports. They were both nice and always talked to me. They let me come to their house and play with their giant dogs. They became by far the best neighbors we have ever had.

Reflections

- Who were the best neighbors you can remember ever having and what made them so special?
- If your parents were not available to help you, who did you rely on for help when you were elementary school age?
- Do you remember any neighbors who had unique pets or lots of animals?
- Can you remember any childhood experience when you became aware of God's presence?

More of the Story:

As I got to know several of the kids in my neighborhood and many even started to come to Kids Bible Club at my house, I discovered that many of them did not like my two neighbors. They would even call them names behind their backs.

What I saw was how helpful these two women were to everyone. They were always busy doing stuff for the neighbors. I just could not figure out why anyone would not like them. Therefore, I asked some of the kids why they didn't like my neighbors.

The kids told me that my neighbors with the giant dogs were "gay" and that I would go to hell with them if I were nice to them. I really did not know what gay meant. In my family, if you didn't know something you could always ask. But I think answering this question was a little difficult for my mom.

I told my mom that some of the kids told me that our neighbor ladies were gay. She shyly explained to me what that meant. She told me about heterosexual relationships and homosexual relationships. Mom shared with me that being gay was a matter of strong conflict among Christians. I do not remember her ever telling me if one view was right and the other wrong. She just told me that for some people it was such a strong issue of conflict that people often got very angry over it.

After Mom explained to me about the gay issue, I was no longer concerned about the neighbor women. They were our friends. But here in Chattanooga religious issues are often discussed in public school and we even get to pray. One of my neighborhood kids brought the gay issue up to my second-grade schoolteacher. He asked her in front of the entire class that if someone was gay would they go to heaven.

My schoolteacher told us the Bible taught that God's plan was only for a man to be married to a woman. She told us about the Bible story of Adam and Eve. She said gay people would not be of God and would definitely go to hell. She was my public schoolteacher and I felt she had to be telling me the truth or she would lose her job. I left school that day with a determination to never again associate with my neighbor ladies.

At supper that night, my dad's supervisor and his wife were at our house. During the meal my dad and his supervisor told us that they'd had the opportunity to play with our neighbor ladies' dogs. I informed everyone at the table that I hated the neighbor ladies.

This shocked everyone because I had always been very close to these women. They wanted to know why I felt that way. I told them what my schoolteacher had said. I explained that she could not lie to her students or she would lose her job. I shared with them that my friends all hated them, too. I told them I was afraid that if I were nice to them God would send me to hell.

Reflections

- Who was your second-grade schoolteacher? What do you remember most about that teacher?
- Who do you think will go to hell, if anyone?
- What do you think about the teacher talking about the gay issue in a public school?
- What other issues do you think cause conflict among Christians? How do you think Jesus wants us to handle such conflicts?

More of the Story:

Well, after my shocking announcement about hating my neighbor ladies, I spent the rest of the night being educated about many things. We talked about hell and what it really was. We talked about what teachers should and should not do. We talked about how wrong hating always is and that God is all about love. We talked about the whole gay issue again. Maybe those discussions were helpful to my parents and dad's supervisor. For me, I was more confused than ever.

I was confused about why there were heterosexual people and homosexual people. I was confused about why some people said my neighbor ladies were going to hell and others said they were God's children. I was confused about why Jesus just did not handle the whole situation himself instead of making me have to worry about it. I just wanted to pass second grade. I really did not care anymore if my neighbor ladies were gay or not. I really did not care if being gay was good or evil. I just wanted the whole situation to go away. I decided that if I did not bring it up again, maybe no one else would bring it up either. I also decided that I would be nice to my neighbor ladies because being nice to people was the right thing to do.

However, my plan to just ignore the whole issue failed. A few weeks later, I was sitting in our neighborhood clubhouse out in the timber near the Tennessee River behind my house. I was there with about a dozen other boys. It was Halloween time and we were all talking about how we were going to terrorize our neighborhood for Halloween and what costumes to wear for trick or treat. Most of the talk was just harmless kid stuff, but then things began to get a little sticky.

The subject of my neighbors came up again. Most everyone at the clubhouse was convinced that being gay was evil. Therefore, they began cooking up plans to punish the women. The plans included throwing eggs at their car, putting potatoes in their exhaust pipes or sugar in their gas tanks, and even giving the giant dogs antifreeze to drink. I knew the plan was wrong, and I told the kids I was not going to be a part of it.

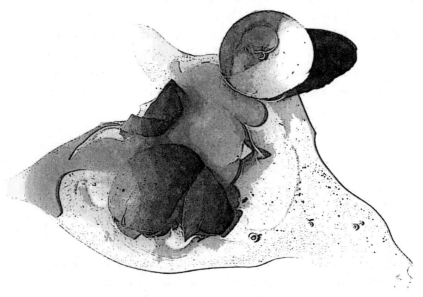

They began to call me names and tell me I was going to go to hell. I was told if I did not want to help them get the "wicked lesbians," then I could no longer be a part of the neighborhood club. I said OK and left.

I never did say anything about the clubhouse talk to anyone. My plan was just to ignore the whole issue and mind my own business. If being gay was a sin then maybe the neighbor women deserved to be punished. If my neighbor clubmates were going to be mean to the women, it was not my fault because I sure was not going to help them. I convinced my little eight-year-old self that I could just ignore the whole situation and focus on other things.

But when it came time for me to go to bed and my family was sharing together in our nightly family devotions, my neighbor ladies and their giant dogs came back to my thoughts. I still kept quiet about the mean plans that I had heard being planned. I said my prayer and went to bed. I was still going to stick to my plan of just ignoring everything.

Reflections

- Did you have a neighborhood clubhouse when you were growing up? If so, what memories do you have about it?
- What were some Halloween tricks that you did?
- What would you do if you were Jared? Just ignore the plans? tell your parents? something else?
- What are your reactions to the neighborhood boys' plans of terrorizing the women? Why do you think the boys were so willing to punish them?

The Rest of the Story:

When I was lying in bed, my neighbor ladies and their dogs kept coming to my mind. I felt that maybe if I prayed about the situation Jesus would let me go to sleep. So I got out of bed and knelt down by it. I closed my eyes and asked Jesus to make sure the right thing happened. I asked Jesus that if the women needed to be punished, to help that happen. I asked Jesus to let my friends do the right thing. Then I got real personal with my Savior. I asked him to let me know what I should do about my neighbor ladies, if I should avoid them or not.

After praying, I felt better and was excited about finally getting to sleep. In my young mind, I had put Jesus on the scene and was no longer involved. I pulled my covers up tight and began thinking about basketball. But three words kept popping into my head over and over and over again: *love your neighbor*. If those words came to mind once that night, they came fifty times. Finally, I fell asleep. When I woke up the next morning, there were those three words greeting me again. *Love your neighbor*.

I ran into the living room to tell my mom about those three words and how many times I had thought about them during the night. She told me about Jesus teaching his disciples about the two chief commandments: "Love the Lord, your God, with all your heart, might, mind and strength; and *love your neighbor* as yourself."

After talking to Mom for a little bit, I knew that those three words were the answer to my prayer for my neighbor ladies. No matter who or what they were, I was supposed to love them and want happiness for them just like I wanted happiness for myself. I told my parents about the plans I'd heard at the clubhouse. My dad immediately went into action to head off anything mean happening to my neighbor ladies.

Later that night the women came over to our house. I was so happy to see them. I ran up to them and gave them a great big hug. *Love your neighbor*—those three words gave me the freedom to enjoy all the good things about my neighbor ladies. Together, they and my parents were able to make sure that none of the mean plans of the clubhouse could be carried out.

For me, a real miracle occurred. I knew that I was supposed to love my neighbors and do whatever I could to help them be happy. Those three wonderful words have blessed my life ever since. The so-called gay issue, which brings so much conflict and pain to others, is really no issue for me. I am not called to be either a judge or a fan. I am called to love unconditionally. I hope I will always be found having the courage to *love my neighbors no matter who they are.*

I have known since second grade that I am supposed to love people and help them be happy. I am supposed to invite people to Jesus and into the waters of baptism. I am called to lift up folks who have fallen down. I am called to bring light to those who walk in dark valleys. I am called to love the unlovable. I am called to be bold in loving my neighbors regardless of their lifestyles. Please pray for me that I will always be brave enough to love my neighbor.

I am supposed to be a witness of the love of Jesus to everyone. If a person is rich or poor, I am called to witness to them of Jesus' love. If a person is smart or stupid, I am called to witness to them of Jesus' love. If a person is right or wrong, I am called to witness to them of Jesus' love. If a person is black or white, I am called to witness to them of Jesus' love. If a person is a saint or a sinner, I am called to witness to them of Jesus' love. If a person is gay or straight, I am called to love them with the unconditional love of Jesus Christ. I hope as I grow from a teenager to an adult, I will always have the guts to love my neighbor with the same love Jesus has given to me.

I realize this experience might not mean anything to those of you who read my story. It is my story and my experience. I am stuck with it. You are not. You do what you need to do, but as for me, I will love my neighbors regardless of their GPA, their race, their religion, or their sexual orientation.

Final Reflections

- Where do you think those three words, "Love your neighbor," came from on the night Jared heard them?
- Reread the last four paragraphs above. What is your honest reaction to Jared's reflection? Do these paragraphs cause you to lose or gain respect for the author, and why?

- How does the author's experience affect your personal view of the so-called gay issue?
- Please pray for those who are in conflict and face pain due to this issue.

What I've Learned

First of all, I want to take this opportunity to tell readers my heart and compassion is with you. I am only a teenager. I lack much wisdom and knowledge. I know this whole subject is a two-edged sword. However, my writings are about sharing some of the experiences that have shaped me as a member of a church-planting family usually ministering on the edges of society. With faith and courage, I shared my experience. It is my experience and I alone will be held accountable for its lessons. As a disciple of Jesus, I've learned from my mentors that we cannot ignore tough issues but must have the guts to talk about them.

Second, I want my readers to know that I do not know, even now as a teenager, if my neighbor ladies are gay. They have never spoken of it to me. No one I ever talked to has had any evidence that my two good friends are gay. People assume they are because they are two single women living together and sharing a life.

Their sexual orientation is really none of my business. They have since moved from our neighborhood, but they are still my friends. They have probably attended more of my basketball games to support me than anyone else besides my parents.

I will tell you with all my heart that if I discovered that they are gay it would make no difference to me or decrease the love I have for them. They are my friends, my best neighbors ever, and my sisters in Jesus. I am proud to have had their influence on my life.

I am only a teenager. I honestly do not know if being gay is a sin or not. I have listened to all the arguments. In school, I have had to debate on both sides of the issue. We each have to respond to Jesus in our own way and to the best of our understanding. As for me, at this point in my life, I will love my neighbors and witness to them about my awesome Jesus. I will be willing to play them one-on-one in basketball. I will break bread with them, and I will share in worship with them, no matter who they are.

My parents have taught me to try to be a minister of righteousness instead of rightness. Rightness may be black and white. Righteousness causes us to have to listen, study, pray, seek to understand, support, and be strong in love. Being right is probably much easier than being righteous. In my attempt to do this, I might be wrong. But I hope to always be found boldly loving my neighbors even if I do not agree with them or fully understand them. *Love your neighbor.* Those words hold me accountable and call me to rise above my own views and try to be brave enough to seek understanding more than judgment.

03
Pillows versus Guns

Here in Chattanooga, one of our three church mottos is *"Our victory lies in our invitation."* We teach all our members, participants, and friends that we are called always to invite others to come with us to church. I have been taught since I was born that if we are unwilling to invite others weekly, we will fail in our calling of fulfilling Jesus' great commission to go into all the world, baptizing them in the name of the Father, and of the Son, and of the Holy Ghost. Therefore, inviting people to church events is always a victory and has become a way of life for me.

Often when you invite someone to church and they accept your invitation, you have the responsibility of picking them up and bringing them to the activity as well as taking them home. This means sometimes you have to spend more time on the road, risking car accidents, flat tires, car trouble, missing the late-night basketball scores, and other minor mishaps of inconvenience. One time, taking an attendee home from church got me into a situation that I sincerely pray no one will ever have to be in again.

I am talking about one of those situations that your church member manuals, Sunday school classes, missionary training classes, and World Conference discussions just don't cover. Maybe it is because you have to be on the front line of hard-living/hard-core ministry and be blessed with my Munson luck for these types of incidents to be a reality. But believe me, once you've lived through one, you'll sure wish somebody had prepared you for it.

Reflections

- Do you consider yourself a lucky or an unlucky person? Why?
- What would you say is the motto of your church congregation?

- Who was the last person you invited to a church activity? Did that person come?
- How do you normally get to church: drive, walk, ride public transportation, ride a church bus, ride with family or friends?
- What do you think the author means when he says "hard-living/hard-core ministry"?

More of the Story:

Greg and I first got acquainted with each other in Little League baseball. One summer we played on the same team. However, Greg did not get to play much, so his baseball career lasted for just one summer.

We got together again in middle school and this time we began to form a friendship. My parents and I decided in seventh grade to take me off the medicine Ritalin that I had been on since I was seven for my ADD (attention deficit disorder) learning disability. The decision was a good one, but for a while I got into a lot of trouble at school. In fact, I became a regular at after-school detention. Each time *I* was in detention so was Greg.

Our teachers' attempts to discipline us allowed Greg and me to form a friendship. This friendship was again interrupted when I stopped getting detention. We had no classes together. I was a jock and spent most of my time hanging with other athletes. Greg did not play sports or attend sporting events. Therefore, we never got to be with each other.

Greg and I finally got to renew our friendship in high school. We were in the same English class and assigned to the same "reading group." Our English class was split up into four groups. I cannot remember their politically correct names, but in teenage terms, one group was for the really smart kids, one was for the "kind of smart" kids, one was for the average kids, and one group was for the dumb kids, who read poorly. Each group was called by a color. Greg and I both had the wonderful privilege of being placed in the "purple" group, which just so happened to have all us "dumb" kids in it. In this group, we formed a friendship and a contact that lasted throughout my high school years.

I need to catch you up a little on my friend Greg. He comes from a violent family. His dad was shot and killed when Greg was an infant. At the time of this story, his mom was still in prison on drug charges, as was his older sister. Two of his three older brothers have been in prison, too. Greg is the only member of his immediate family who has never been arrested.

His one brother recently got off probation and his other brother has been in and out of trouble with the law but has not done any prison time. Greg lives with these two brothers and his grandmother.

One of Greg's dreams is to be the first member of his family to reach the age of twenty-five without a criminal record. However, he fears this will not be easy for him because of his family background. When your family has a reputation for being troublemakers, cops and teachers seem to think any member of the family is bad. Besides his family reputation, he is also small in stature and gets picked on a lot. Sometimes he is picked on so much that he loses his temper, thereby causing him to react in some unhealthy ways. I had seen Greg fight a few times over the years and never saw him lose a fight. But Greg knows that eventually fighting will cause him to end up getting hurt or going to jail.

Reflections

- Were or are you a good student in school? Were or are you considered a good or poor reader?

- Did you ever get detention in school? If so, do you remember why? How did your school primarily punish students?
- Do you keep in touch with any of your school friends?
- Did you ever get into a fight at school? If so, what happened and why?
- Have you ever invited a school friend to church? What happened due to the invitation?

More of the Story:

Finally after years of trying and inviting, Greg agreed to start coming to a cell church that was meeting in my home. Through this cell group, our friendship grew even stronger through our mutual desire to serve Jesus. But neither of us could have predicted what was about to occur following his first-time attendance at a church event.

Besides doing the regular cell church stuff, our cell church played a new game called "holey board." It was a game that I learned at a summer camp in Illinois. This game sometimes lasts longer than expected, especially when beginners are playing. The length of the game resulted in Greg needing a ride home.

As I drove him home, this tough street-fighting teenager shared his heart with me. At the age of sixteen he felt I was the only person in school who liked him. I was the only person who ever invited him to church. He shared his dream of remaining crime free.

In that short ride from my house to his, he shared how much he wished he could believe in God. He said no one had ever told him about God. He said he loved cell church and hoped he was welcome to come back. Of course, I told him he was always welcome to come back.

As we pulled into his driveway, Greg made another surprise request. He said, "Nobody has ever prayed for me before tonight. I hope this doesn't make me sound like a pussy, but it felt good when your dad prayed for me at church tonight. Do you pray Jared? If you do, could you pray for me again? I hate going home."

If I knew what was going to follow my prayer, I honestly would have said no and backed my Chevy Blazer out of his driveway as quickly as it would go. But I said yes and offered a prayer for my friend. After the prayer, he made another request. He asked me to come in and meet his grandma and pray for her because she had just got out of the hospital from a surgery. I turned my truck off and walked into Greg's home for the first time ever. I did not know I was walking into a dangerous situation.

Reflections

- What was your first vehicle?
- How are you feeling about Greg so far in the story?
- Do you know anyone who has never been "told about God"?
- Have you ever been asked to pray for someone in his or her driveway? Where is the most unique place you have ever prayed for someone else out loud?
- What "dangerous situation" do you think awaits Jared and Greg?

The Rest of the Story:

We walked into Greg's house. His grandmother was sitting in a chair near the television set. Greg and I sat near her on a big sectional couch, with gobs of pillows covering it. As we sat down in the living room, I kept hearing voices yelling at each other. Sometimes they were so loud I could not focus on our chatting.

I had been there for only a few moments when I heard Greg's brother running down the hall shouting, "I am going to shoot the son of a bitch's head off." Greg told me to get out of the house.

But before I could get up and leave, Greg's brother came into the room with a handgun and started firing shots into another room. Then the other brother began firing back and hit the first brother in the arm. Blood was flying.

I do not know what I was thinking, but I grabbed the pillows off the couch and began throwing them at the gunmen. I just stood there throwing pillows and yelling at the two men to grow up. *What was I thinking?*

Finally, the gunfire stopped. Greg's grandmother went to the phone and called 911. Greg ran to his wounded brother's side and I just sat back down on the couch. I guess I was in shock. It is not every day you bring someone home from church and get to witness a shoot-out between brothers. It also is not every day that a teenager gets to defend himself against gunfire by stupidly throwing pillows.

The grandmother told the brothers I was a minister or some type of a preacher. She then asked me to pray for the family. I was slow to get off the couch, unsure what to do or to pray for. I was not sure it was safe. But I finally got up and stood by the wounded brother along with the rest of the family, including the shooter.

My crazy night was not over yet. I asked this family to pray with me by repeating the prayer. We call it the Chattanooga style of praying. The strangest thing I remember about this night was that after the shooting was over, everybody was friendly to each other. It was an experience that scared me sick, but they acted like it was no big deal.

When the police arrived, they came into the home with guns drawn. They shouted for us to raise our hands. I didn't realize they meant for me to raise my hands, too. I guess shock had taken over my brain cells. I just froze. One of the cops pointed a gun at me and told me to put my hands up. This time I got the message and my hands went up. This became the third time in my life that a police officer had pointed a gun at me.

Emergency workers went to work on the wounded brother and police began questioning the rest of us. Of course, they did not believe I was there as a representative of Jesus. How many times do you hear about teenage ministers anyway? And how many times do ministers show up at a gunfight? It took several minutes before the police were convinced that I was *not* the bad guy.

I had to write out a statement of what happened and what I heard, saw, and did. When the police heard about me throwing pillows at the gunmen, they gave me a long lecture—the same lecture I heard from both of my parents later that night. I could not leave for a while but they did let me call my dad. However, I was given permission to leave before my parents could show up.

I was never so glad to get home. Once I had a shower and got in bed, I began to realize how blessed I was not to have been shot. I was feeling nervous for some reason and could not relax enough to go to sleep. So I got dressed, moved the cars out of our driveway, and played basketball till 3:30 in the morning. Finally I went inside and fell asleep.

A few days later Greg came to our house after school. He asked my dad and me if we would help him find God. He said the shoot-out and my ability to throw pillows and talk strongly to his brothers with no fear convinced him that he needed Jesus in his life. I quickly told Greg that I was scared to death and had no idea why I stood there and threw pillows at his brothers. He responded that he knew it was because Jesus was by my side. I jokingly replied that I wished Jesus had thrown a few pillows in my place.

After a few more moments of talking about the shoot-out, Greg again asked us if we would help him find God. He was very sincere. Since that day Greg, Jesus, and I have become very close. I baptized Greg a few days later.

But the real blessing for me came through a personal commitment Greg and I made to each other. As was mentioned earlier in this story, Greg wants to become the first member of his family *not* to have a criminal record at the age of twenty-five. Well, I, too, have a dream that I shared with Greg. I want to earn a bachelor's degree through a college education. My grandparents, my parents, all my aunts, and all my uncles do not have a bachelor's degree. My family heritage is not rich in college education but very wealthy in love, realness, and courage.

Greg is afraid his life circumstances and his temper will keep him from achieving his dream. I, too, am afraid that my learning disability and poor study habits will keep me from being successful in my efforts to earn a college degree.

However, Greg and I have promised to pray for each other daily. So far we both are keeping our promise. This may sound strange, but there are times when I feel Greg praying for me. Besides my parents, Greg is probably the only other person on the face of the earth who prays for me daily. I consider myself very blessed to have a brother in Christ like Greg.

At the time of writing this, Greg has committed to enlist in the Marines and is working hard to reach his dream. I have committed, after high school, to attend Graceland University in Iowa where I hope someday to earn a bachelor's degree. We both have hopes and fears in our decision to reach beyond what most people think is our potential.

Isn't God neat? God used a dangerous gunfight and a stupid incident of throwing pillows to allow Greg and me to know that we will not be totally alone in our efforts to reach our dreams. We both have Jesus, the Community of Christ, and each other's prayers.

I am so glad I kept inviting Greg to church with me and that Greg invited me to his home. We both experienced new things. I experienced a family who uses guns to settle arguments. Greg experienced a church family who uses love to face the hard knocks of life. We both gained the strength that can only be found through the family of Jesus Christ. Please, if you read this story, stop and pray that my brother Greg can remain crime-free and safe.

Final Reflections

- What are your overall reflections on this story?
- Has your relationship with Jesus Christ blessed you with good friends? If so, in what way?
- In the story the author says, "I feel Greg praying for me." What do you think he means by that? Have you ever felt someone praying for you?
- Have you ever witnessed or experienced a gun battle? If so, how has it affected you?
- Both teenagers, Greg and Jared, mentioned having dreams they hope to accomplish. What is one of your dreams? Does this story help you in your dream-seeking in any way?
- Please pause right now and have someone pray for Greg and Jared to be successful in reaching their dreams.

What I've Learned

First of all, I learned never to take pillows to a gunfight. More seriously, I learned not to judge someone based on his or her family's reputation. Most people always considered Greg a troublemaker. I found a true friend and a brother in Jesus in him.

I also learned that God sometimes uses one of the scariest experiences of life to bring peace, strength, and courage. I also learned to have the courage to share my fears. My fear of going to college gave me an opportunity to form a Christ-led friendship with another teenager.

I also learned that there are some people in this world who want to know God but need a guide. I also know there are still some people who keep their promises. Greg is still praying for me daily just like he promised.

How about you? Are you keeping your promises and commitments? Are you keeping Jesus strong in your life? Are you really praying for the people who are seeking your prayers? I know when we are brave enough to try to keep our commitments, we find an inner strength beyond our understanding.

04
White Chocolate

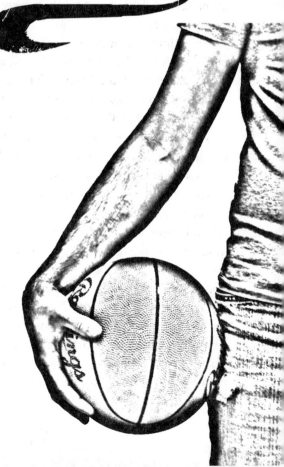

"Hey little white boy, you want to play me in some make it-take it basketball?" Those were the first words I ever heard "Big T" speak. For the next two or three years of my life, Big T and I would play basketball together nearly every day. We were both just twelve years old when our relationship began at a neighborhood driveway where kids gathered to play basketball.

Sometimes we just shot around and sometimes we played one-on-one. Often we would do our best to play basketball at the state park or the YMCA with the older, more experienced guys because we knew that the only way you improve in basketball is to play against guys who are better than you.

Big T had a lot of basketball talent. At twelve I wish I had just half of his talent and a little of his height. It was part of his family heritage. His dad and brothers were all well-known for their basketball skills.

Sometimes when we played at the state park, Big T would have to talk the other guys into letting me play. They did not believe a white boy could hang with them. It was during those days that I received one of my youthful nicknames: White Chocolate.

Big T and White Chocolate got to be teammates not only on the streets but also in some AAU basketball. We played ball together a lot but did not hang out with each other much off the courts. I was usually busy doing church stuff and he was busy surviving the streets. The only thing we had in common was our love for basketball.

As the months passed, T and I got to know each other better. We were even winning a few free lunches by beating older guys in some two-on-two basketball games. But T discovered I was into Jesus and I discovered Big T was into crime. He was put on probation for some robberies he was involved with.

One day during an AAU game, Big T and White Chocolate were sitting the bench together due to our team being so far ahead that our coach gave us starters a chance to ride the bench so other players could get some experience. As we sat there, Big T shared with me that he knew he was heading for trouble.

He told me his only hope of beating the temptations of the streets was for him to be able to play professional basketball. He shared that his PO (probation officer) and counselor thought he was doing good. But he confided in me that he had started partying with a wild bunch and was using drugs a little. He asked me to pray for him. I said OK.

He got quiet for a few seconds and then looked up at me and asked me if I was going to pray or not. I was just thirteen and supposed to be watching my teammates play ball, but instead a buddy needed me to pray. So I prayed out loud as softly as I could for Big T. It was just a short prayer.

You probably know what happened with my old Munson luck: the coach yelled at me for talking instead of paying attention. I could have told my coach that I had been talking to Jesus but I doubt it would have been helpful. We both ended up running laps for our praying experience on the bench that day. Big T would always tease me after that by saying that my prayers just got us in more trouble.

Reflections

- What was one of your youthful nicknames or street names? How did you get it?
- Have you ever been yelled at for praying? Do you think Jared should have told the coach he was praying?
- What is your favorite sport to watch? to play?
- Why do you think Big T felt playing professional basketball was his only hope of beating the streets? Do you think many thirteen-year-olds have experienced drugs or alcohol? What are you personally doing to help kids stay off drugs?

More of the Story:

In the next AAU season Big T got kicked off the team for missing practices and showing up late for games. The streets kept calling to my old basketball buddy. I tried to talk with him a couple times about it. He never got mad at me. Big T would tell me thanks for caring about him and to keep praying for him.

I must confess my praying for Big T did not occur as often as it should. I could make up a lot of excuses, but I just failed to pray very often for my buddy. Once in a while something would cause him to come to mind and I would pray for him, but never did I spend much time of focused prayer on him.

After his dismissal from the team, we didn't see each other much. Occasionally our paths crossed at the mall or a high school basketball game. We even played some basketball together once in a while at the park. But for the most part, we drifted apart.

One night I was at my high school for a basketball game. I was playing varsity ball but was sitting in the bleachers watching the JV game and waiting for it to get over. Big T walked in with some of his new friends. He saw me and came over and shook my hand.

It had been four years since we played our first basketball game together and about a year since we had been teammates. However, we still had a connection. He sat and we talked for a while. Our discussion was mainly about basketball and girls.

As it got time for me to go to my locker room, we gave each other a hug. Big T told me he heard that I was a minister now and said sometime maybe I ought to try to get Jesus on his case. We laughed and went our separate ways.

He stayed for my game that night and we won. I had a pretty good personal game that night also—I scored the winning basket for our team. After the game Big T walked up to me and congratulated me on my basketball performance. He said something to me I will never forget. He said, "White Chocolate, you gotten real good. Basketball and Jesus is going to make you a real winner. Losers like me love to have winners for friends. So remember, we're friends forever." He hugged me and left before I could respond to him due to other folks standing around wanting to talk to me.

Reflections

- The author mentions "focused prayer" in the story. What is focused prayer? Do you have a focused prayer life?
- What is your reaction to Big T so far?
- When was the last time you can remember running into an old friend someplace? Take time right now to pray for an old friend from your past who is on your mind.

The Rest of the Story:

I wanted to see if I could help Big T. His words stuck in my mind that he felt he was a loser. The streets were winning him. I talked to my parents about trying to help Big T. We discussed some options and then had a little family devotion of prayer time on behalf of Big T. I was determined that the next time I ran into him, I would take time to invite him to Jesus and try to help him.

My intentions were good, I guess. But my good intentions failed. Shortly after our basketball game meeting, Big T committed suicide with a gun at his uncle's house.

I got the word from his older brother who called to ask me if I would be the minister at the funeral. I told him I would have to think about it.

I did not feel worthy of doing the funeral. Big T was supposed to have been my friend. I was supposed to have been a minister but instead I was so busy enjoying my basketball success that I did not even take time out to pray for him. I knew he was reaching out for help yet I did not take the time to go find him instead of waiting on some chance meeting. I failed my friend and I felt so guilty.

My parents let me struggle with my guilt for a few hours. Then my dad came into my room to give me a lesson of real ministry. If you know my dad, he can be in your face with the truth and cut you to pieces with it. He felt there was a need for some ministry from me to a hurting and lost family and I was too busy being sorry for myself.

My dad is very accepting of people, but once you accept priesthood responsibility he expects you to always put the lost first. He let me know that my tears and guilt were natural but not a good enough excuse to get out of offering ministry at my friend's funeral. Dad let me know that night I was being called to do ministry, and my pain, guilt, and failures could not stand in the way.

He was right, but dang him—why does doing the right thing have to be so hard sometimes? I picked up the phone and called Big T's family and told them I would be honored to do the funeral service.

It was going to be the first funeral I had ever done by myself. It was also the first time I was going to do a funeral for someone who committed suicide. I was scared. I was in way over my head. I needed Jesus' help but felt so unworthy to seek it.

I asked my parents for help. I did everything I knew to do but none of my preparations seemed to be helpful. Finally I prayed. I asked God to forgive me for my errors in not helping Big T. I asked God to forgive me for being so selfish even now and thinking so much about my own failures and myself. I finally asked God to help me do the funeral in a way that would make Big T happy.

I may be just a teenager but I am a big believer in prayer. Shortly after talking to Jesus in prayer, my thoughts were guided back to my first meeting with Big T: the day he challenged this little white boy to a basketball game. I knew what to do now.

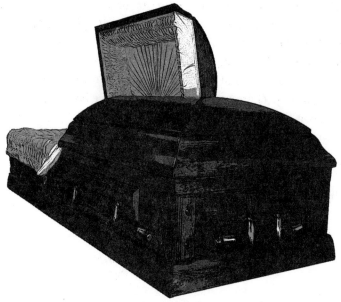

I did not wear a suit to the funeral. Instead, I wore my AAU basketball uniform. I did not carry a Bible with me; I carried my basketball. When it came time for the funeral message, I told those gathered about my good friend Big T. I told them the difference he had made in my life. I told them about how he had helped me become a better basketball player. I shared with them how it was Big T who gave me my "White Chocolate" nickname. I told them about his prayer request as we sat on the bench and how we had to run laps for not paying attention to the game. I told them about my buddy, Big T, coming to my basketball game and telling me how we were to be *friends forever*. I told them about the guilt I felt and that I knew many of them felt guilty in failing to help him. I told them about the forgiving power of Jesus. I told them about life after death and how I knew Big T and I were still friends and that nothing, not even suicide, could ever change that. I placed my basketball in his mother's hands and told her to believe me that her son — my friend Big T — was with Jesus and not to listen to anybody who ever said otherwise. Then we prayed Chattanooga style, with everyone repeating the prayer.

I wish this story had a happy ending. It doesn't. The family members were very kind in their expression of appreciation for my words and my unique style. But if my words were good, they were not my words alone. I am just not good in public/pulpit-type ministry. Therefore if that funeral service brought any ministry, it was the Spirit of Jesus who blessed them.

My friend took his life. I cannot change that. All I can do is remember all the special things Big T did for me. I write this chapter to say thank you to my friend Big T for the rich memories his young life gave to me.

Final Reflections

- How does this experience of reading about Big T and White Chocolate affect you?
- Have you ever lost someone to suicide? How have you dealt with it?
- Do you know a teenager who has taken his or her own life or attempted to? What can we do as disciples of Jesus to increase hope in the lives of teenagers and youth?
- Do you feel Big T is with Jesus? Why or why not?
- How do you feel about Jared's dad's response to Jared's guilt?
- What do you think about Jared's funeral ministry in this story?

What I've Learned

Part of our gospel journey includes dealing with failures. I know people seem to love success stories. However, my parents have taught me that the lessons we learn as we attempt to climb the mountain will strengthen and sustain us much more than the mountaintop experience itself. It is important, despite the pain, for us to realize we will fail and fail in a big way sometimes as we attempt to witness. Failure is not something for us to fear but to face and learn from. We also must not let our guilt and fear of failing keep us from responding to the call of Jesus to bring hope to others.

I also learned to be much more disciplined and focused in my prayer life and to listen and follow up better when people reach out for help. I learned that suicide does not send a soul to hell. Suicide is a choice some people make in this life. It is probably always a poor choice, but it is a choice. I know that Jesus is with us when we make good choices and Jesus is with us when we make poor choices. For me, I believe that when someone makes the poor choice of suicide, Jesus is still there with them being their savior and best friend.

05
Popcorn in a Drug House

A little child shall lead them. These words I have heard since my toddler years in Sunday school class. Well, this is an experience that came about because of the faith of a little boy.

Tyler came to Bible Club every time we had it. I was serving as the teenage pastor of this little kids' Bible Club consisting of four-to-seven-year-olds. Usually sixteen to twenty kids came each week, but Tyler came every time.

He was a tough little African-American boy who took no hassle from anyone. I must admit that I enjoyed tormenting him at times just to see him get upset. His facial expressions when he was angry were adorable. He was also very protective of his little sister and often got into some trouble when he felt another kid was messing with her.

Every week at Bible Club we had a "me too" time. "Me too" was the period when the kids got to express things they were concerned about and the group would support each other by praying together the words "me too." Each time, Tyler would say how concerned he was about his mom and her "smoking stupid crack dope."

Tyler's mom was in and out of jail often. Tyler spent most of his time with his grandmother. He would often say, "My granny is a good person but my mom needs Jesus to kick her dope-smoking ass." This saying would always make the other kids laugh but Tyler would always be upset with their snickers.

Tyler loved to eat popcorn. His grandmother used his love for popcorn to reward him for good behavior. If Tyler got in trouble at school or at home, he did not get any popcorn that night. But on the days he was trouble free, he would get rewarded with a large bowl of popcorn.

One time at Bible Club we were having popcorn as our snack and Tyler did not take any. He told me that he did not deserve popcorn because he had said some bad words earlier. I told Tyler that in Jesus' house our sins are forgiven if we ask Jesus to forgive us.

Tyler wanted to know, if he told Jesus he was sorry for the bad words, whether he could eat popcorn. I told him he could. He bowed his little head and told the other kids to shut up so he could pray. He then prayed and told Jesus he was sorry for the bad words he had spoken earlier and promised to try not to cuss ever again. As soon as he said "Amen," he said, "Give me some of that damn popcorn." I couldn't help but laugh.

Reflections

- Do you have any experiences of being led by a little child?
- How do you like your popcorn? What is your favorite snack food?
- Have you ever had a problem with cussing? Where do you think Tyler learned his cussing?
- Have you ever made a promise to God and quickly broken it? Why do you think we do that?
- Did your parents have problems with addictions—alcohol, drugs, sex, work, or other?

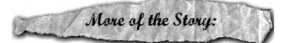

More of the Story:

Bible story time had just ended. Tyler, who was seven years old at this time, said to me that we needed to talk. I sat down on the floor and Tyler sat near me. He said he had been praying for his mom for years and nothing had gotten any better. "Jared, does Jesus hate my mom? He ain't helping her yet. Maybe Jesus doesn't love our family because we're poor."

This seven-year-old then confronted me with my own calling as a disciple. He said that in the Bible stories, Jesus' helpers always brought people to Jesus. He wanted to know why I and the other ministers had not brought his mom to Jesus. He added that if there were real disciples of Jesus in the world today they would go and drag his mom to Jesus.

My heart ached for the pain I knew little Tyler was feeling and yet I sensed his deep love for his mom. His faith in Jesus and his "real disciples" was also easy to notice. I was moved by our discussion but I cannot remember my response.

When it came time for Bible Club to end, I rode with Dad to take Tyler and his little sister home. As we were driving, Tyler asked Dad if we wanted to go by and see the place where his mom stayed. Tyler said the place was a drug house for "stupid dope smokers."

As we drove by the house, Tyler asked if we could stop. He wanted to know if Dad and I would go inside and get his mom. He said that he would pray for Jesus and his angels to go with us to protect us against the pimps and dealers.

Tyler said if we were real ministers for Jesus that we would not be afraid. I asked Dad what we should do because I felt so helpless for Tyler.

Reflections

- What would you say to Tyler if you were in this situation? What would be the best action for Jared and his dad to take?
- Have you ever been to a drug house? Do you know of any drug houses in your neighborhood?
- What do you think is the difference between a disciple of Jesus and a "real disciple"?

The Rest of the Story:

Dad pulled the car over to the side of the road. He took hold of Tyler's hand and talked to him. Dad explained to Tyler that there had been several times we had tried to help his mom. Dad told Tyler that his mom would not let us help her.

Tyler screamed at my dad, "I don't want *you* to help her, asshole. I want *Jesus* to help my mom!"

Dad talked further with Tyler in words that a little inner-city street boy could understand. He promised Tyler that after he dropped Tyler off at his grandmother's house, he would go back to the drug house to talk to Tyler's mom again. Dad asked Tyler to promise to pray real hard for his mom—harder than he ever had. Tyler promised that he would. We then pulled out and drove Tyler home. Tyler seemed very confident that my dad's visit would bring success in reaching his mom.

I told Dad I wanted to go to the drug house with him. It took some convincing but he agreed to let me be involved. We placed a phone call to our pastor and Dad asked him to come to the drug house, too. While we waited for our pastor, my dad and I both prayed for the situation.

Nearly thirty minutes later our pastor pulled up. I thought we might discuss some plans for our visit to the drug house but we didn't. We just went to the front door and knocked. A guy opened the door and asked what we wanted. Dad told him we were there to talk to Tyler's mom. The man said she was busy, and Dad said to the man, "Well, she just better get unbusy." Dad then pushed his way into the house as my pastor and I followed him.

As we entered a room full of people, Dad turned to me and told me to go back to the car. I could tell by the look on his face that it was not a good time to argue with him. I turned around and walked back to the car. I waited for what seemed like forever.

During my wait, Dad's cell phone rang twice. The first call was from my mom. I was glad to hear from her and I told her what was going on. She told me she would call me back in ten minutes. The second call was from Tyler's grandmother wanting to know what was going on.

Before my mom could call back, the front door of the drug house opened. My pastor was the first person out. Following him were my dad and Tyler's mom. They walked to the car and Dad told me to call Mom and tell her that we were going to have a house guest. I jumped into the back seat and called Mom.

When we got home, Mom helped Tyler's mom get settled in her room. Dad told me to call Tyler's grandmother. I dialed the number and handed it to Dad, then listened to Dad's side of the conversation. Dad finally handed me the phone and told me to talk to little Tyler while he went to get Tyler's mom to come to the phone.

My chat with Tyler was brief. Tyler said he prayed super hard for his mom. He told me he now knew Jesus really did love his family. He was so excited. Tyler told me that he would be eating popcorn for the rest of his life because he was going to be a good boy forever.

Tyler's mom spent about a week at our house. She then entered into a long-term drug rehab program.

As I write this story, Tyler and his mom have both been baptized. Tyler still struggles with cussing and his little temper flare-ups. Tyler's mom has completed her rehab program and is now working in a nursing home. She is studying to be an LPN (nurse) and is also a cell-group leader for our church.

She is doing great but is very busy. She, Tyler, and his sister all live with Tyler's grandmother. They still have a lot of ups and downs but they are doing great. She and Tyler are very bold about telling everyone how Jesus saved her from hell by having ministers drag her out of a drug house on the night she was thinking about killing herself.

No matter what anyone else thinks, Tyler's family is convinced that God sent us to that drug house that night. They are also strong witnesses of the power of prayer. They are great inviters. The cell group that Tyler's mom is leading has already resulted in two baptisms.

Final Reflections

- What is your reaction to this story?
- Would you have gone into the drug house that night?
- What do you think gave Jared, his dad, and their pastor the courage to go after Tyler's mom that night?
- Do you know anyone who has been successful at staying off drugs or alcohol?
- What role do you think the power of prayer played in this incident?
- Why do you think Tyler's mom is willing to be a cell-group leader and a strong inviter? How can we help you to become a stronger inviter?
- Pray right now for Tyler's family and their continued safety and success.

What I've Learned

I learned from this experience that God really does change lives when people care enough to help each other. The faith of a little child is a powerful thing.

Sometimes we must give our prayers some legs. If my dad and pastor had not had the guts to risk that night by going into the drug house, Tyler's prayers would not have been successful. Disciples must be a people of action for the prayers of the seekers to be answered successfully.

I also learned to never underestimate our own courage as we respond to the leading of God's Spirit. I've learned to listen to the wisdom and courage of children.

I guess maybe the most important thing I have learned is that we must be bold in our actions of winning the lost. Too often in our attempts to be wise, play it smart, and be safe, we hesitate to take action. Action always requires faith and guts. We also must learn to never give up on people even if they have given up on themselves.

06
Mental Illness in Algebra Class

Algebra II class in high school was an interesting experience. I had a brand-new teacher who suffered from a nervous breakdown before the semester ended. I made an "A" in it by some miracle. Yes, you read that right. I made an "A" and it was a greater miracle than the parting of the Red Sea. It was a miracle partly because I got kicked out of that class at least once a week.

Several of my closest buddies were in the class with me and our teacher would kick us all out of class at the same time. Somebody would make a smart remark and she would kick our whole group out of class. Often it was not even one of *us* who made the remarks. But if someone made a noise or threw a paper wad, she would kick one member of our group out of class. When the rest of us protested her unfairness, we would all end up being sent out of class.

She seldom sent us to the office. She just told us to get out of her class and we did. Sometimes we would go to the office ourselves to tell our principal what had happened. But most of the time, we just walked the halls.

I used our time of walking the school halls to begin to tell my buddies about Jesus. My algebra teacher did not know it but she was an instrument in the hands of Jesus. If she hadn't kicked my friends and me out of class, I never would have had the chance to witness to them.

As we walked the halls, I would tell them stories about the life of our church family. It got to be a weekly tradition: we would get kicked out of class and someone would say it was "church time." We would go and sit in the hall and talk about our experiences with Jesus. My friends began to look forward to us getting into trouble so we could do "church time." Before the semester was over, six of my algebra buddies began coming to church with me.

I later had the privilege of baptizing some of these friends into the church. I want to tell you about one of these friends. His name is Maxwell.

Reflections

- Did you take algebra in school? Who was your teacher? What grade did you get in it?
- Did you ever get kicked out of a class in school? If so, why?
- Have you ever had a strange teacher? What was strange about him or her?
- Did you ever invite a classmate or a co-worker to church? Did they come? Did they get baptized?
- What do you think about Jared using the incidents of being kicked out of class as an opportunity to witness of Jesus? Why do you think his classmates called it "church time"? Why do you think his classmates started coming to church with Jared?

More of the Story:

Maxwell was one of those boys teachers just do not like. Probably most teachers would deny having a teacher's pet and probably also deny having a scapegoat student. Despite their denials, it has been my experience that most teachers have their pets and their goats. Maxwell was a goat and especially our algebra teacher's goat.

No matter what happened, Maxwell would be the one who got in trouble. There were even times when Maxwell was not in class and somebody would throw something. The teacher would yell at Maxwell and tell him to get out of class. But he wasn't even there! When you get kicked out of a class you're not even in, something is strange.

Maxwell became one of my best friends. Most of the time when he got in trouble in algebra, I was one of the next to suffer the teacher's wrath. This algebra adventure allowed Maxwell and me to begin to share many things.

Maxwell used to be a pretty good student in our younger years, but things changed. I never really knew why until our algebra "church time."

Maxwell's mom suffers from mental illness and she was in a mental hospital most of that semester. She has been suffering from mental illness for years. She would go out in the middle of a highway and try to direct traffic. She also believed there were people living inside the walls of their house and so she would cook the "wall people" meals. She also purchased television sets and other expensive items to give to the wall people. This caused some deep financial problems for Maxwell's family.

All these things caused Maxwell to lose self-confidence and self-esteem. Teachers didn't seem to help his situation at all. No matter what Maxwell did, it was wrong and not good enough in the views of most teachers. His drive to succeed began to be lost and his grades suffered. Maxwell began living with the fear that he too might have mental illness. This fear led Maxwell into a lifestyle of drugs and violence.

Through our algebra adventures, I got to find out why the changes had occurred in his life. But I found out something more important about Maxwell. I discovered he was a very talented teenager. He was funny, smart, a musician, and he wanted to get closer to Jesus. I also found a great friend in Maxwell.

Reflections

- What are your views of Maxwell so far in the story?
- Do you agree with Jared that most teachers have a teacher's

pet in their classrooms? Do most teachers have their scapegoat student whom they always seem to blame for things?
- Maxwell has a fear of becoming mentally ill because of his mother's mental illness. What fear do you have or have had as a result of a family situation? Do you know someone who suffers from mental illness?
- How do you feel the teachers could help Max? How could Max help himself? How could Jared help? How could the church help? How could Jesus help?
- Have you ever known someone who was labeled a troublemaker but was actually a very gifted person? Have you ever been mislabeled or misunderstood?

More of the Story:

I invited Maxwell to come to church with me. At first he always had an excuse of being busy or something. I cared about my friend and was not about to let his refusal of my invitations keep me from getting him to Jesus.

I kept inviting. His refusals and excuses stopped. He began to tell me that the people who make the most fun of him and put him down the most were usually church folks. He said every time he went to church with someone, he would feel out of place. He shared that he usually got in trouble when he attended church.

Knowing his fears, it was easier to witness to him. Our congregation is made up of people who have been abused by other Christians and do not always behave or respond in traditional ways. Our uniqueness as a local church family was helpful in persuading Maxwell to come. I kept inviting him, and he finally agreed to come and give it a try one time.

That was all it took. Once Maxwell came to church with me, he found a family and a place where he fit in and could grow. Maxwell's talents were appreciated and put to work. He is loved by everyone in our congregation. He walks in and the whole place lights up. Everyone's spirit is lifted because they know Max will put a smile in their heart.

Even with Maxwell and me now going to church together, along with some of my other classmates, our experiences with our algebra teacher did not improve. It got worse, especially for Maxwell.

Our teacher began to bring a tape recorder to class to record all the remarks and sounds that she believed were being made in class. One day, one of our classmates took the tape out of the recorder and attempted to throw it out of the room. But instead of landing out of the room, the tape hit the wall and landed near Maxwell's desk.

Everybody began laughing at our classmate's bad aim. Our laughter caught our teacher's attention. She saw the tape lying near Maxwell and began yelling at him, accusing him of stealing her tape. Maxwell bent over and picked up the tape. He started to bring it to her desk.

As Maxwell approached her desk, the teacher lost control of her temper. She struck Maxwell across the face twice. She then began yelling and cussing at the whole class, demanding that some of her students leave the room and go to the resource officer's office.

Of course, all my friends who had started attending church with me got kicked out along with me. Without going into a lot of details, this whole thing ended up in a giant mess. Maxwell was totally innocent, at least this time, but the teacher was demanding that he be expelled from school.

All of us had to write out what we saw and heard. The resource officer and the principal interviewed us all. When the mess was all over, Maxwell got to stay in school and our teacher was fired. By the way, we all passed Algebra II.

Maxwell got the reputation of being the kid who got his teacher fired. The kids thought it was cool but Maxwell felt it would just add to his bad relationships with teachers. This whole deal caused him to hate school even more.

Reflections

- What do you do when someone you invited to church says no? Do you give up or do you invite again?
- Maxwell's experience with church kids showed they were more mean spirited than other kids. Do you agree or disagree with his experience?
- Have you ever seen a teacher hit a student? a student hit a teacher?
- Have you ever been blamed for something you didn't do? What happened?
- Does the experience with the teacher in the algebra class surprise you or not?
- How do you think you'd feel if you were Maxwell?

The Rest of the Story:

I got to baptize Maxwell into the body of Christ a short time after our teacher was fired. Maxwell's dad came to his baptismal service and wept. He said the year had been real tough on Maxwell and Maxwell felt no one loved him. He said that Maxwell had already changed since he started coming to church with us.

I have had the wonderful experience of baptizing several people in my young life. Being able to baptize my dear friend Maxwell was awesome. I keep most of my personal experiences with Jesus private. But I want to humbly share what occurred to me when I baptized Maxwell.

As we got into the horse tank that we use as a baptismal font, Maxwell and I were laughing because we were so cold. When I raised my hands to say the baptismal prayer, I felt a great joy within me. I am a very happy person but this joy was different from any other joy. I said a silent prayer: *Thank you Jesus for this moment. Maxwell is my friend and I am so glad you brought him into my life.*

Well, to my surprise, after my short silent prayer, these words came to my mind: *Jared, Maxwell is my friend, too. Thank you for inviting him into my house.* It was so real and yet I wondered for a moment if I was not suffering from mental illness myself because now I was hearing a voice in my head.

A few weeks after Maxwell's baptism, we were at a church camp together. Maxwell shared with me that on the day he got baptized, he heard Jesus say to him, *Maxwell, I love you, and thank you for responding to the invitation given to you.*

I then shared with Maxwell my experience with the words I heard in my mind that day. We both talked about our experience for a bit then both concluded that we might be suffering from mental illness since we were hearing God in our hearts and minds. We decided that if feeling that happy is what mental illness is like, we could handle it.

Maxwell has gotten off drugs and has become a strong participant in our church family. He shares a powerful testimony of Jesus and invites many people to church. He has even introduced his mom to the church and she has formed a relationship with the Community of Christ. She has since gotten out of the hospital and returned home. She is working again and things are much better for this family.

Maxwell wants to become a minister someday. He reaches out to many people and even has given the "message" at Sunday celebration a few times. The most amazing thing is that Maxwell often prays for our algebra teacher who was fired for hitting him.

He is still struggling with school. He is still afraid of mental illness, but he is not letting this fear hold him back. On the day I am writing this chapter, Maxwell and I are going to be chaperoning a bunch of inner-city kids from our church to their first circus experience ever. Maxwell made all the arrangements and got the tickets for the kids.

Teachers might see Maxwell as a troublemaker, but Jesus and I see him differently. Maxwell is a strong disciple of Jesus. He cares about people and faces his fears with the faith that he will never be alone because his friend, Jesus, and the Community of Christ family will be there with him. Our God is an awesome God!

Final Reflections

- What do you think about Jared and Maxwell's experiences at Maxwell's baptismal service? Did they hear God's voice or was it just their imagination? Are they suffering from mental illness and hearing voices? Have you ever felt God was talking to you?

- Jared talked about feeling a "joy" at Maxwell's baptism. Have you ever felt a special joy at a baptism or other worship experience?
- What do you think contributed to the positive change in Maxwell and his family? If you were Maxwell, would you be praying for the algebra teacher?

What I've Learned

I learned that Jesus really does get happy when people respond to our invitations to come to church and to be baptized. I also learned that we shouldn't judge someone by his or her reputation. Too often we close the door of potential when we choose to trust a reputation instead of taking the time to know someone.

I also learned that just because someone is a trained professional, like a teacher, that does not mean they are always right. They make mistakes, and we have to learn to trust our own judgment.

I found a friend and a fellow disciple in Maxwell. I learned to try to see people as Jesus sees them instead of trusting the views of other people.

I also found out it is important to keep inviting even if the first several responses are "no." Most of all, I learned that Jesus could take a bad experience like getting kicked out of class and turn it into a blessing. Do not judge people based on their reputation. Get to know people first before passing judgment. God is an awesome God and can help them change for the better.

07
Jesus and My Middle Finger

My mom got dressed and ran down to jump into her car at 6:30 in the morning to go to work like she does every Monday through Friday. But this morning's ride to work was going to be very different for her.

As she walked out into the driveway to get into her car, she stopped by the backyard fence to pet and talk to our dogs who had been barking a lot for some reason. As she walked toward the car she noticed four young teenage boys standing near the timber next to our house. She figured the boys were the reason for our dogs barking.

She backed her car out of the driveway but realized that she had left some needed paperwork on the kitchen table. She pulled back into the driveway and as a result was now running late. In her rush, she left her car door open and ran into the house.

When she came back into the house, I asked her where a permission slip for a school field trip was. She had forgotten to sign it, so she handed it to Dad to take care of and headed back out. She was now several minutes late as she got back into her car.

She started to back out of the driveway when she noticed something in the back seat—a very unwanted passenger. Somebody had put a snake back there. This was not the first time a snake had been used to frighten my mom. When I was very small and we lived in Illinois, somebody dumped a bag of snakes on our front steps, but that is whole different story.

Needless to say, when Mom saw the snake, she panicked and hit the brakes. She jammed the car into park and got out as fast as she could. Once safely in the house, she demanded that Dad "Get that monster out of my car. Just do it. Just get it done. Shut up and do it."

Dad and I had no idea what she was talking about, but it was clear that Mom was upset. I started to run out to the car but she grabbed me, demanding that Dad get to the car first. Dad looked inside but didn't see anything. Mom and I followed him out and by then Mom was much calmer.

She told my dad there was a snake in the car. He looked in all the windows and finally saw it on the back-seat floor under the front seat where the snake probably had landed after my mom jammed on her brakes. Dad got a shovel then opened the door. Mom and I immediately ran back into the garage as if the snake were on a mission to attack us.

We peeked out of the garage just in time to see the snake on the end of Dad's shovel. Dad threw the snake back into the timber. Mom wanted to know why Dad did not kill her unwanted passenger. Dad said the snake was probably as scared as she was. Well, I don't think Mom was convinced or even concerned that her unwanted passenger was frightened.

Mom refused to take her car to work that day. Therefore, Dad let her borrow the church's car after he looked under its seats and in the trunk. Mom then left for work. Dad and I, now laughing about the whole incident, got into Mom's car to take me to school. I think I was in the third or fourth grade.

But Dad couldn't get the car out of park. Something had broken in the gears of the car as a result of my mom's desperation to get away from the snake.

I got to stay home from school and Dad had to call a wrecker to come get the car. I don't know what was wrong with it, but I know it cost a few hundred dollars to get it fixed. This would not be the last time some strange things happened at our house.

Reflections

- What time does everyone normally get up at your house on a weekday? Who is the first member of your family to get up?
- When was the last time your family had to call a wrecker?
- Do you like snakes? Where was the most surprising place you ever saw one?

- How do you think you would react if you were driving your car and saw a snake in it? If you were Jared's dad, would you have killed the snake?
- Have you ever gotten out of your car or truck and left the doors open as you ran inside someplace?
- How do you think the snake got in the car?

More of the Story:

A few days after the snake incident, my family went back to Illinois to visit my grandparents for a weekend. When we pulled back into our driveway from our trip, we noticed that my mom's car had two flat tires. As we examined it closer, we saw that the tires had been cut.

Several times during the years, when my family has taken a trip, on our return home something bad had happened to our house. Even today when we leave for a trip, we worry about what we will find when we get back home.

Not only had the tires been cut but the car had been scratched. Again the repairs cost a few hundred dollars. My dad would jokingly say he wished those things had happened to the church car instead of the family car because the church would be paying for the damages instead of us.

On another occasion, somebody poured some white paint all over our dogs. We had a "beware of dogs" sign hanging on our fence but our dogs were far from dangerous. They barked a lot but if you walked up to the fence, they would jump up on the gate so you could pet them. Well, our so-called watch dogs got themselves painted white and the paint had dried on them, so we could not wash it off easily. One of the dogs appeared to be sick so we took the dogs to the vet.

Yeah, you got it. It cost my folks a few hundred dollars to have our dogs tended to. But the final straw came following another experience caused by neighborhood vandals.

Somebody broke into our garage and this time they went too far. They did not take anything that belonged to my parents. This time they took my stuff! They stole all my basketballs, my baseball glove, my football, my Dennis Rodman basketball jersey, my tennis shoes, my "Duke" hat, and some other less important items.

Now *I* was upset. We had turned each of these incidents in to the police, but outside of making a police report, no results had come from the professionals. I felt it was time for me to take action. The previous incidents, even though they did cost my folks a lot of money, had not affected me that much until now.

After all, our neighborhood vandals had given me the opportunity to miss a day of school, an opportunity to see what my dogs would look like if they were white, and a chance to learn how to change a flat tire. But now they had messed with the wrong nine-year-old. Taking my Dennis Rodman basketball jersey was the unpardonable sin, in my young mind.

After expressing my anger to my parents, I came up with a plan. Step one: I would get my very best friend, Jesus, on the scene. After all, Jesus knows everything, including who the vandals were. Step two: I would talk to all my friends and we would do some of our own police work. Step three: after we found out who the vandals were, I would tell my dad on them and then they would be sorry.

Reflections

- What precautions do your family members take to protect your home when you are gone on a trip?
- Have you ever had a watchdog? How good was the watchdog?

- Has your home ever been broken into? Have you ever been robbed? How did being a victim of a robbery make you feel? Have you ever broken into someone's house? Have you ever robbed someone?
- What would you have done differently if you were in the Munsons' shoes?
- What do you think of Jared's three-step plan? What do you think of Jared's statement that Jesus knows everything?

More of the Story:

I immediately put my plan into action. I went up to my room and knelt down by my bed. I talked to Jesus about the whole incident. We always prayed for his protection and I knew that we were safe because really it was just stuff that had been damaged or taken. But I told Jesus I *really* wanted my Dennis Rodman jersey back in a bad way.

The next morning I contacted all my neighborhood buddies and told them what had been happening. Well, one of my buddies told me he bet it was a kid named Roberto. He said Roberto belonged to a gang and his family hated preachers.

Great, the first two steps had worked out perfectly. Now it was time for the third step: telling my dad and letting him take action. With great excitement and pride in my own investigating, I told Dad what I had found out. I couldn't wait for him to bring justice to the situation. Maybe I would get my Dennis Rodman jersey back after all.

My enthusiasm was quickly squelched. Dad said we had no way to prove it was Roberto and it was probably best if we just let the police handle it. I couldn't believe it. My dad, who usually charges into hard situations like Superman because of his mistrust of professionals, wanted to trust this to the professional police. I was crushed by his decision not to take action.

The first two steps had gone forward so easily and now we were standing still when it was so obvious who the bad guy was. Well, the next day my neighborhood buddies wanted to know what my dad did with the results of our investigation. I told them that my dad didn't do anything nor had plans for any action.

My buddies and I were not just going to accept such inaction. We *knew* Roberto was the criminal and needed to be brought to justice. He was fifteen or sixteen years old. We knew that he could beat up any one of us. But we decided that if we all confronted him, he would confess his life of crime.

Therefore, my ten-year-old neighborhood friend, my five-year-old neighbor twin boys, and I boldly walked down to Roberto's house. It was going to be four against one. We were confident that the victory would be ours. But when we got to his house, he was sitting on his porch throwing a knife into a tree. When my twin neighbors saw his knife, they ran home before we could stop them. Now the odds were two to one but still in our favor.

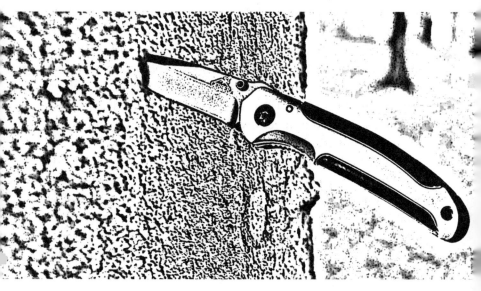

Before I could say anything, my remaining buddy courageously took charge of the situation. He shouted, "Roberto, you better stop stealing from Jared or he will kick your butt. Jared ain't afraid of your ugly face."

Roberto quickly stood up and ran toward us. We boldly turned around and ran as fast as we could back to my house because it was the closest. We now stood bravely on my doorsteps with my dad just inside if we needed him. Roberto was threatening and yelling at us. We yelled back, and then we did a very immature thing — we gave him the finger. You got it. We flipped him off with the double barrel action of both middle fingers on our hands.

My Munson luck was cursing me again. My dad stood looking out our front door and saw me doing the finger thing. Before I knew it, I had been grabbed and lifted to my front room couch. My dad was all over me. The "bad guy" got away and I was now in trouble. Life just is not fair.

As I tried to explain my position with all the reasoning that any great defense attorney has, it soon became apparent I was not going to be happy. First, my dad explained to me exactly what the middle finger being extended meant. I already knew what it meant but felt it was wise just to be a good student and let Dad teach me. After a very long lecture and some youthful tears, my dad gave me my punishment. I had to go to Roberto's house, knock on his door, and apologize to this sixteen-year-old thief for my action of flipping him off.

I couldn't believe it. I was the good guy here. My stuff was stolen. I was the victim yet I was the one who had to knock on the door of my enemy and say I was sorry.

I walked down the street with my dad following close behind me. My buddy was waiting for me. I stopped and explained to him what I was doing. He agreed to walk with me and I was so glad. I walked up to Roberto's house. I knocked on the door. He came to the door and I quickly made my apology and turned and walked away.

But my ordeal was not complete. My dad told me he was proud of me for being brave enough to say I was sorry, but flipping people off was a childish act. Silently I was thinking that since I was a child maybe it was OK for me to do such a childish thing. But after I spent the rest of my night writing, "I will never flip any person off again" about 500 times, I knew that flipping people off was not going to be a profitable action for me.

Roberto was stealing and vandalizing my family. He got to be with his friends. I had to stay inside and write that stupid statement over and over again. Boy, I was going to get that Roberto someday, no matter how long it took.

Reflections

- Have you ever "flipped somebody off"? Has someone ever flipped you off?
- Do you think it was fair of Jared's dad to make Jared apologize to Roberto for flipping him off? Was it fair to make Jared write the statement 500 times?
- What would you do about the Roberto situation?
- Can you understand Jared's desire for revenge? Have you ever done something to someone out of revenge?
- What do you think will happen between Jared and Roberto? Do you think Roberto is probably the thief and the vandal who had been harassing the Munsons?

The Rest of the Story:

Unknown to me at the time, my dad then went to Roberto's home and confronted him about the stolen items, the snake in the car, and the other incidents. Roberto denied everything. My dad's visit to Roberto's home upset Roberto's mom.

She came to our house and wanted to know why my dad was accusing her son. During their discussion and my dad's explanation of the whole situation, Roberto's mom said she thought Roberto might be the guilty person because he had some of the items we were missing. Sure enough, her investigation resulted in Roberto confessing to all the incidents.

Roberto's mom also told Dad that she was a nude dancer. She informed him that over the years she had been verbally abused and attacked by several ministers who disapproved of her career. Roberto had grown up with a great dislike of ministers due to their judgment and poor treatment of his mom. She was certain Roberto's action was due to my dad being a minister.

Roberto gave back all the items he stole except one. He had given my Dennis Rodman jersey to his girlfriend and she used it to sleep in. Just my luck, the one item I wanted back the most was now a part of some teenage girl's lingerie collection. Boy, did I want to get that Roberto.

At the time of this taking place, my dad was holding cell church meetings at 1.a.m. on Mondays at a local strip bar. After the club closed, Dad would do church with strippers, bouncers, and their families. During those years, this church event resulted in several baptisms and about twenty strippers deciding to get out of the lifestyle. Dad invited Roberto's mother to get involved with this cell church group.

She did become involved in the church group and Dad baptized her a few weeks later. After Roberto's mom got involved in the life of the church, she insisted that Roberto get involved, too.

Not only did I have to live in the same neighborhood with the thief of my favorite jersey, now I had to go to church with him. My life sucked.

One night I got fed up with going to church with Roberto and I told my parents it wasn't fair. Well, both of my parents gave me a lesson about my need to welcome everyone to church, especially those who are thieves and troublemakers.

In my family we have the freedom to express how we feel, but this privilege also means we have to listen to other family members about their views of our feelings and consider following their advice. My family decided that I needed to pray twice a day to ask Jesus to help me forgive Roberto and learn to like him. It was also decided that I needed to be brave enough to tell him my feelings.

I began that very night praying for the ability to forgive Roberto. The next cell group meeting I was at with Roberto, I shared with the whole group my feelings about him. As I explained that I did not like Roberto and did not trust him, I also shared that I knew Jesus did love him and that I was praying for Jesus to help me learn to forgive him.

Roberto got up and walked over to me. I looked over at Dad for protection because I did not want to be beat up. Roberto knelt down and looked me in my eyes. He told me that he was sorry. He told me that he respected me because I was a kid with a lot of guts.

Roberto shared with us that he was a gang member and wanted to get out of gangs but was afraid. He said, "If I had Jared's guts, I could walk away."

In that very moment I forgave Roberto and he became my friend. With the help of several people, Roberto was able to walk away from gangs. We became good friends.

Dad baptized Roberto and his family became very active in church. Roberto started to work as an oil changer at a garage and the garage owner sent him to mechanic school. Roberto became a mechanic. Today he is a manager of an auto repair shop about twenty miles away from Chattanooga.

Roberto was happy to be able to provide for his family and was proud of his mom for quitting her nude dancing and becoming a waitress.

At the time of writing this chapter, I have since been ordained and Roberto has fallen in love. He and his fiancée have asked me to perform their wedding ceremony.

Isn't God awesome? The thief who put a snake in my mom's car and stole my favorite jersey is now my brother in Christ and wants me to share in his wedding. Only the power of prayer and the love of Jesus can cause enemies to become brothers and friends.

If none of my other life experiences have been evidence of the life-changing power of Jesus, this experience is. My one-time enemy is now my friend and brother in Jesus. What my dad says is true: God sure does a lot of neat stuff.

Final Reflections

- Has an enemy ever become your friend? How did it happen?
- What do you think of doing church services at a strip bar with strippers? Would you want to be involved in this type of ministry? Why or why not?
- Why do you think Roberto and Jared became friends? Do you find any experiences of courage in this chapter?
- Have you ever honestly confronted someone with your bad feelings about them? What happened in the relationship when you did?

What I've Learned

I learned so many things from this experience that I am not sure I can list them all. I learned that it is important to be bold and to share your true feelings with others. There are too many things in life that are fake. Our relationships should not be based on pretending and unrealness. We need to love each other enough to be honest with each other in a loving way.

I also learned that people do change. In my young life I have seen so many so-called "bad guys" become great and kind people just by being touched by Jesus and the Community of Christ. When you believe that people can change, it is much easier to find the courage to witness. I wonder if part of the reason people are slow to witness of the love of Jesus is because in our hearts we do not really believe Jesus changes people. For me, I know the love of Jesus changes lives daily.

I also know we must pray for our enemies. We must pray and ask God to teach us to forgive. I gained a friend because of my ability to forgive someone for stealing my Dennis Rodman jersey. I learned that having Roberto as a friend is a better gift than any basketball jersey.

I also learned that even the people who do bad things to us could be won to the gospel if we respond to those situations as disciples of Jesus with love instead of revenge. If we learn to love even the unlovable folks in our lives, we can become successful disciple-makers and real peacemakers.

08

Messin' with Shootist

"Bang! Bang! Bang! Bang!" is the sound that a ten-year-old boy called "Shootist" will never forget. This was the sound of the small-caliber handgun he used to shoot the man who was beating and raping his mother.

As the oldest son in the household, Shootist knew his job was to protect the family. When the man, a street pimp, was hurting his momma and she was crying out for help, he did the only thing he knew to do. He took the small handgun from his momma's dresser and fired it at the attacker until the man fell to the floor.

This experience resulted in Shootist being "gone from the hood" for a few years. Nobody really knew whether he went to juvenile detention, jail, foster care, or a mental hospital. He just was gone after this incident. When he returned to the neighborhood four years later, he had earned the street name of Shootist.

The word on the street was he earned that name from the shooting incident. But he always claimed he got his street name from his granny, whose favorite movie was John Wayne's last movie, *The Shootist*. It really didn't matter where his street name came from; it was his name and what everyone knew him by.

I did not know him until his return to the neighborhood of our church center. He was now fourteen and most folks were afraid of him because of his reputation. He didn't come to the center for worship celebrations. He just came to play basketball and was very quiet. No one ever messed with him or gave him any hassles.

As we began to inquire from the other kids what was up with Shootist, we learned about his story. Everyone just said, "Don't mess with him. He's dangerous. He's always got a gun with him."

Reflections

- Have you ever personally known a pimp or a "street-working lady"? What is your opinion of people who make their living this way?

- Do most people know you by your real name or a nickname? If a nickname, where did you get it?
- How many guns are in your home? Have you ever fired a gun? How old were you when you first fired a weapon?
- What is your opinion of Shootist so far in the story? Do you believe that some fourteen-year-olds here in the United States carry a gun on them often? How does it make you feel that some teenagers have access to handguns? One of the ten commandments is "Thou shall not kill." Do you feel Shootist broke that commandment by shooting a man who was beating his mother?
- How do you think your congregation would handle someone carrying a handgun to church?

More of the Story:

After finding out the possibility that Shootist might be carrying a gun to the church/center, our pastor and my dad confronted him about it. I don't know what took place in this conversation. I just know everyone was reassured that Shootist would not have a gun with him anymore at the church or at any of our activities. Also, posters went up at the center advising participants to make sure they do not carry weapons, illegal drugs, or alcohol onto the property. The other result from this conversation was that Shootist began coming to worship celebrations and teenage church, but he never participated verbally.

Between worship experiences, there is always a basketball game going on at the center. I've played basketball all my life and have been taught to play the game with great intensity and competitiveness. However, usually at the center I am much more relaxed in my playing style. But one day we were involved in a really intense game. Shootist and I were playing on opposing teams, guarding each other in a man-to-man defense. There is always a lot of trash talk going on. One thing led to another and Shootist and I got into a little scuffle.

As we were being pulled apart from each other, I realized I was being silly and offered my apologizes to Shootist. He was still upset with me, however. He wouldn't back off because his temper had now taken over. He was escorted outside and was asked to leave, which is the policy at the center if we are unable to apologize to each other after a conflict. He finally left, vowing to come back with a gun and put a "tap in my ass."

The neighborhood kids were certain that Shootist was going to keep his vow of violence. Of course, word of the conflict got to my pastor and my dad. As always, we discussed many options quickly. We could ignore it and see if Shootist would just calm down. My pastor and my dad could get involved and go talk to him and his mother. I could go home and just forget about the whole mishap and hope that distance and time would allow everything to cool off. I could go outside, wait for his return, and see what would happen. I could stay inside the center, see if he came back, and go from there.

Reflections

- Have you ever been playing a game when someone got upset and became violent? If so, what happened? Do you get angry when someone is cheating in games or sports? Have you ever personally gotten so upset at a game that you lost your temper?
- Do you consider yourself a competitive person in sports or games?

- When you are involved in a conflict, how quickly do you apologize? Do you usually apologize first or only after someone has apologized to you?
- Have you ever told someone you were sorry and then your apology was not accepted? How did this make you feel?
- If you were in Jared's shoes in the incident, how would you handle the threat from Shootist? What do you think Jared did?

More of the Story:

Before we could make a decision, Shootist sent his younger brother into the center to ask me to walk across the street to just talk to Shootist. Before I could say anything, my dad spoke up and said, "You tell Shootist if he wants to talk, to be a man and walk over here and talk to Jared here at the center or just go away until he is man enough."

The younger brother said that Shootist could not come to the center because he had a gun and knew it would be taken away from him if he came to the center. Dad got up and went outside. Nobody would let me out of the center. They all blocked the door to keep me inside.

A few minutes later, Dad and Shootist walked into the center together. Shootist looked at me and told me he wanted to fight me but not with any weapons. I told Shootist I would fight him if he wanted me to, but that we should settle it on the basketball court instead of with fists since it was basketball that got us in the situation.

After a few moments of lively discussion, it was decided we would play a basketball game of three on three, and he could pick the teams from among the teenagers. The stakes were if I won, Shootist would start reading the Bible during study time and take a more active part in worship celebrations. If his team won, we would have a fistfight. Everyone felt this decision was the best, except for my mom. She felt the whole thing was stupid and that we needed to just hug and make up. But Shootist was not having any of that idea.

The game was going to be played and before it started nearly every kid in the neighborhood had gotten word of the game and its stakes. The center was packed full.

The teams were chosen and the rules were set. We would play three-on-three basketball of "make it-take it" and no fouls called. The winning team would be the first team to score twenty-one by ones, and you had to win by two points (baskets).

Again the stakes of the outcome of the game were reviewed and agreed on by both Shootist and myself. The other four players agreed to play their best for their chosen team and to do their best to make sure everyone honored the rules and stakes of the game. It was all settled now. If my team won, Shootist would agree to take an active part in our Bible study class and take a leadership role in worship celebration. If Shootist's team won, we would go to the playgrounds and fight.

To start the game, my dad had three of the neighborhood kids pray about the situation and the safety of the game. Several kids volunteered to pray but only three were chosen. As their prayers were being offered, I was offering my own prayer that I could play my best. I was confident that I could win the basketball game but also confident that I could win a fistfight if it came to it. But I must admit, I was a little afraid that the fight wouldn't stop with just fists. The prayers were said, and Shootist's team got the ball first.

Reflections

- What do you think about the basketball game solution? What do you think about the stakes of the game?

- What do you think about the adults at the center allowing such a game to take place? Do you agree or disagree with the adults' decision to allow the game to be played?
- How would you be feeling if you were in Jared's shoes?
- What do you think about the decision for prayers to be offered before the game? If you were offering a prayer before this situation, what do you think your prayer would be?
- Do you think if the fight occurs it will just be with fists or do you think a weapon might get used?

The Rest of the Story:

The game began and it was pretty rough. It was not the roughest and most physical game I have ever been in, but it was definitely more physical than most basketball games because no fouls could be called.

For the most part, it was not much of a game. My team won easily 21 to 9. But when the winning basket was scored, everyone quickly got a little nervous about what Shootist's reaction would be. He hung his head for a moment, then looked up and stared at me. He walked over to me and stuck out his hand and said, "You are a baller. The next time, I want you on my team."

With that said, he walked over to my pastor and said he was sorry for losing his temper. They hugged and the incident ended as quickly as it began. No guns. No fighting. Just a basketball game among six teenagers was all that occurred. Since then, many conflicts in the center's neighborhood area have been settled with a basketball instead of a fight.

Shootist was good to his word and read out loud at Bible study from then on and did whatever he was asked to do during a celebration service. He slowly became one of our leaders at the center. We became buddies and even teased each other about our fighting game.

Nearly a year later, Shootist asked me to baptize him for Jesus. It was an awesome experience, as is every baptism. But this one was special because Shootist once asked me to walk across the street so he could shoot me and now he was asking me to baptize him. This was definitely a miracle and evidence of how the love of Jesus can calm a storm. Two enemies became good friends because of Jesus. There should be no doubt in our minds that the gospel does make a positive difference in lives, families, neighbors, cities, and countries. I gained a friend, a brother, a co-worker, and a protector because of the difference Jesus and his gospel made in Shootist's and my life. God is awesome.

Final Reflections

- What is your reaction to this experience between Shootist and Jared? Have you ever had an experience where an enemy became a friend?
- What do you think about Shootist asking Jared to baptize him? Why do you think he did that? Who baptized you and why did you ask this person to baptize you? Who was the last person you saw being baptized? How is that person doing today?

- How have you seen the gospel of Jesus make a major, positive difference in a life?
- Share with each other ways you see God as being "awesome."
- Have someone offer a prayer of thanksgiving for the positive changes the gospel of Jesus makes in people's lives.

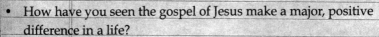

What I've Learned

I have learned there are alternatives to fighting and violence. I've learned that Jesus really is the Prince of Peace and he will bless us in our peacemaking efforts if we are willing to be bold risk-takers.

I have also learned that the gospel of Jesus Christ really can bring people together and help them become friends and brothers. I have learned that baptizing anyone is a giant turn-on and excitement builder, but baptizing a former enemy is the most awesome privilege in the world.

I learned that basketball could literally be a lifesaver for me. I also learned that most people are not nearly as bad as their reputation sometimes makes them out to be. And sometimes, my strong desire to win on the basketball court can get me into trouble.

Probably the best lesson from this experience is how the love of Jesus can take a bad situation and bless it with his touch, turning it into a miracle of great joy. The gospel does make a difference and it is worth our attention.

In talking to Shootist about sharing this story, he made one request: He did not want people to think of him as a bad guy. I want all the readers to know that our brother in Christ, Shootist, is a great guy. He serves God weekly at the center and is a great peacemaker. He, just like me, is still a teenager and faces challenges. But he loves Jesus and works hard to be a positive witness.

09
An Issue of Blood!

Whenever you are actively trying to do missionary work and church planting, new opportunities for ministry and helping others come your way. This is the story of one of those opportunities for ministry that comes along due to no effort of your own beyond trying honestly to live your faith. It is important to remember that faith is not *part* of a disciple's life; faith *is* a disciple's life.

I was sitting in my sophomore English class and had just completed taking a test when a girl placed a note on my desk. I grabbed the note quickly because I did not want my teacher thinking we were cheating on the test. I put the note inside my notebook.

But as my Munson luck goes, another student saw me hiding the note. Just like some immature, grade-school tattle-telling brat, this teenage classmate yelled out, "Michelle and White Chocolate are passing love notes."

I couldn't believe it. First of all, it was none of her business. It certainly could not have been a love note. I did not even know this Michelle. She was a junior who had to take tenth-grade English over, and that was all I knew about her.

Now the whole class thought we were passing love notes. Everybody was chuckling and I had to find a way out of this mess. The teacher asked me for the note. I did the only thing I knew to do. I lied. It was just one of those little white lies people talk about, but it was still a lie. Yes, I was already an ordained minister, but I still lied. I did not need to have my teacher think I was cheating; my grade in that class was already low enough. I also did not need any rumors about me and some girl going around. I had been a victim of rumors and outrageous lies from a former girlfriend already and didn't want to have to face new rumors. So I chose to lie. Yes, I know it was a sin, but I lied anyway.

I claimed there was no note and that my classmate needed to learn to keep her mouth shut. Michelle also denied any knowledge of a note.

It worked. The teacher believed us and gave the class a speech about tattle-telling as if we were in pre-school Sunday school class. As soon as the bell rang, I dashed out of the classroom and never took time to read my mysterious note.

Reflections

- Have you ever been caught passing a note in school? What happened?
- Were you ever a tattle-tale? Who was the tattle-tale in your family as a child?
- Have you ever been hurt by rumors? How did you handle it?
- What was the last "little white lie" you remember telling? Have you ever lied to a teacher? Have you ever lied to stay out of trouble?
- What do you think of Jared telling that lie about the note? What do you think the note said?

More of the Story:

I forgot all about the note in my notebook. I think maybe a little of my ADD kicked in and I lost focus about the whole note incident. I went through the remainder of the school day and never gave the note a second thought.

I went home from school to get ready for a basketball game. I think most athletes are a bit superstitious. I always eat a Blimpie sub before a game. When I fail to do so, it seems like my game is not at its best. I know it's silly, but silly or not, I learned not to take any chances when it comes to my basketball performance. I had a Blimpie sub before every game that season.

I was sitting with a couple of my teammates. We were eating our sandwiches and talking about the upcoming game when one of them asked me what the note said, because he was in my English class. I told him that I had forgotten to read it.

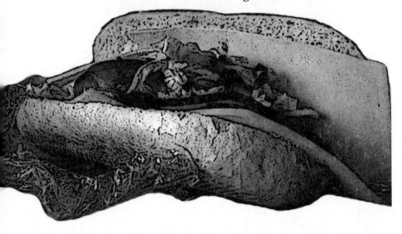

Of course, they didn't believe me and started teasing me that it *was* a love note. Even at the game that night my teammates told me I was going to have a hot hand because I was in love again. I did have a good night on the court. We won, and I did have a hot hand and was the leading scorer for the night.

When I got home, I went to my room and got the notebook out of my book bag. I found the note and opened it. I read it to myself. The note said,

> Dear Jared: I hear that you believe in God and are some type of a minister. I guess I believe in God too but I do not pray. Will you pray for my dad? He is in the hospital and is dying. Please pray for him. Please. — *Michelle*

After reading the note, I must admit I felt a little guilty about my own selfishness all day. But there was no time to focus on my little bit of guilt. A sincere request for prayer had been made. The request came from an almost complete stranger who exercised her courage and faith in placing the note on my desk. I had to go into action.

I went to my parents' room and showed them the note. I told them I felt bad about not paying any attention to it. They simply said that I could pay attention to it now. We did a family prayer service for Michelle, her dad, and the whole situation.

My dad was leaving town in the morning for a weekend ministry trip somewhere. I wanted his view about what I should do as a follow-up ministry to the note. We discussed some options.

- Can you remember a time when your family had a family prayer service? How often does your family pray together now? At meals? at bedtime? only during a crisis? never?
- What is one of your superstitions? Do you believe in luck?
- What do you think about Michelle's note? What do you think about Jared's response to it?
- What follow-up plan of ministry to the note would you use if you were in Jared's place? Do you ever make an on-purpose follow-up plan in your own personal witnessing opportunities?

We came up with a plan for follow-up ministry for me to take in the morning. I got undressed and went to take a shower. While standing in the shower, I again felt compelled to talk to Jesus about Michelle's request. While I stood there in the shower, I felt that waiting until the morning was too long to wait for follow-up. I felt something needed to be done right then to let Michelle know that her prayer request was being honored.

I got out of the shower, dried off, and went to the telephone. I began calling some of my friends to see if any of them knew what Michelle's last name was and if they knew her phone number. It was after 10 p.m. but I knew most of my buddies were still up and Jesus was wide awake, too. Somehow, between Jesus being on the scene and the large network of my buddies, I knew we would find Michelle.

Finally, one of the phone calls paid off. One of my buddies' girlfriends knew Michelle and got her phone number for me. It was then after 11 p.m. but I wanted Michelle to know her prayer request was being honored. I called the number and her brother-in-law answered. He told me that Michelle and her three older sisters were all at the hospital with their dad.

Earlier in the day, I did not even know who Michelle was, but since the note incident I had discovered a lot about her. She had guts enough to place a note on my desk based on my reputation. I had found out she did not pray but that she did have enough faith in God to ask for prayer help. I found out her dad was dying. I found out her phone number. I found out she had three older sisters. And I found out she was sleeping at the hospital. Suddenly she was not such a stranger to me anymore.

I went and asked my dad if he would go to the hospital with me right then. He agreed and we jumped in the car and headed to the hospital to see a girl whom I had never even spoken to at school. One thing I knew for sure — it was going to be an interesting weekend.

As we arrived at the hospital, we were directed to the ICU. When we walked in the waiting room, Michelle and a woman were playing cards. She looked up and saw me. She said, "Jared, are you looking for me? I hope so." I nodded my head in the affirmative.

She ran over and hugged me. She introduced me to her three sisters and I introduced them to my dad. Michelle explained to her sisters who we were and that we were ministers. The oldest sister informed us that they were not religious but said, as she pointed across the waiting room, "but the bitch over there is a religious fool."

This surprised both dad and me. I was glad Dad was there, as he took the lead in the talking. He did not even respond to the sister's comment. We were sharing in a few questions about how their dad was doing when Michelle spoke up and insisted that we go pray for her dad. The oldest sister went across the room and spoke to the woman whom she had pointed to earlier.

On her return to our side of the room, she simply said, "OK, let's go pray for Dad." When we got to the room, Michelle's dad was in a coma. Dad asked me to offer a prayer out of our religious tradition for the ministering of angels and then he anointed the man's head with oil and prayed for him, again out of our religious tradition.

I noticed during the prayers that all four sisters were crying. I also noticed that the woman from across the room had come into the room. After Dad finished praying, the oldest sister asked Dad if we could go to the hospital coffee shop to talk. Dad agreed.

As we walked to the elevator, the woman from across the room meekly went back to the waiting room while we all got on the elevator. The oldest sister poked her head out of the elevator and said, "Good. That bitch ain't coming."

As the elevator door closed, Michelle looked at me and said, "Thank you for coming Jared. You are a special guy. We got a damn *blood issue* happening here."

Reflections

- Where is the strangest place you can ever remember praying? Have you ever prayed in the shower or bathtub?
- What time is too late for you to make phone calls? What time is too late for you to receive phone calls?

- What do you think caused Jared not to wait until the morning to do follow-up?
- Have you ever heard someone pray for the ministry of angels? Why do you think Jared's dad anointed the man's head with oil and then prayed? Have you ever been blessed by having your head anointed with oil and a minister offering a prayer for you?
- Have you ever had a close family member die?
- Who do you think the woman from across the room is? Why do you think the sisters are angry with her?
- What do you think the "blood issue" is? Can you remember any time in the Bible when a woman had an issue of blood and reached out to Jesus?

More of the Story:

As we sat in the coffee shop, we found out more of the story. The woman across the waiting room was their stepmother of just two years. The oldest sister was in her thirties and Michelle was the youngest sister, but none of them had lived with their dad for nearly fifteen years.

He had come to the hospital for a needed surgery. During the surgery he lost more blood than was expected and needed a blood transfusion but that was against his wife's religion. Without the transfusion, he would die.

I had never heard of a religion that did not believe in a blood transfusion but Dad was familiar with the belief. We spent about an hour and a half in the coffee shop with the sisters. Finally, we all went back to the elevator.

When we got back to the ICU waiting room, Dad asked me to stay with Michelle while he and the oldest sister went to talk to their stepmother. Michelle and I talked about school stuff. After a period of time, the stepmother and Dad walked over to us. Dad asked me if I wanted to pray one more time.

We all went to the room and Dad had us repeat the earlier pattern of prayer again. He explained to the group of women that he would be gone out of town for ministry reasons for a few days. He boldly told them that if they needed anything just to call me.

Dad and I left and discussed the whole incident as we drove home. We hugged each other goodnight. When I woke up the next morning for basketball workout, Dad had already left on his trip. I got up, lifted weights, and then left for basketball workout.

When I got home from workout, I called my pastor and asked him if he would go to the hospital with me to see Michelle and her family. Of course he agreed. When we arrived at the hospital, our timing was either right on or poor because Michelle's dad had just died a few minutes before we arrived.

Her oldest sister was yelling at their stepmom, calling her a murderer. To add to this stressful situation, Michelle ran to me and slapped me across the face. She shouted, "I hate you. I hate people who pray and go to church. I hate f---in' God most of all!" She then ran into the ladies' bathroom.

I cannot ever remember being slapped across the face before, unless maybe from my parents when I was smarting off to them. I did not know what to do. My pastor suggested that we walk down to the chapel and pray for a few minutes and then come back up. That is what we did.

When we arrived back upstairs, the hospital social worker was with the family. Michelle saw me and quickly walked over to me. I felt I was going to get slapped again and was thinking how I would respond if her open hand came flying toward my face.

Instead of slapping me, she hugged me. She told me she was

sorry and that she really did not hate God or me. We finally got a chance to pray with the sisters.

The oldest sister told us there would not be a funeral but that their stepmother was going to have a private service at her house and the sisters were not going to attend. Instead they wanted to have a private service for their family and wanted me to preside over it. I boldly suggested that my dad or my pastor would be happy to do it and I could help them. But they insisted that they wanted me to do it, and so I agreed.

The next surprise was that they wanted to do the little service on the next afternoon, which meant I would not have much time to prepare. Praise God that my pastor was with me, and he helped lead us through all the arrangements.

As we left the hospital I was thinking how rapidly my weekend had gotten strange. On Friday morning, I was minding my own business trying to pass an English test when some girl I had never even spoken to wrote me a note. The note resulted in me spending Friday night at the hospital with people I did not know. Now my Saturday resulted in getting my face slapped and being cussed out. On the next day, I had to do a funeral service for a man I did not know, with a family who said they did not like religion, ministers, or even God. This was something my dad could handle with ease, but for me it was harder than playing one-on-one against a guy six foot nine.

Reflections

- Have you ever heard of blood transfusions being against someone's religion? What do you think about the stepmother's decision to stay true to her religious belief even if it meant her husband was going to die?

- Do you think she was a murderer or a hero of the gospel? What do you think about the daughters' reaction to their stepmother?
- Have you ever hated God? Has anyone ever told you they hated God?
- Has anyone at school or work ever asked you to pray for someone? How did you respond?
- Have you ever been slapped across the face? How would you have responded to the slapping if you had been in Jared's shoes?
- How tough would it be for you to do the funeral service in this situation?
- In what ways do you see God's presence in this experience? Do you think it was a coincidence that Jared and Michelle had the same English class or do you think God used the situation to bring a blessing?

The Rest of the Story:

My mom helped me prepare my comments for the service. I decided to use the story of the woman who touched the hem of Jesus' garment as my main story.

The funeral service went pretty well. It was held at a park. My pastor led the group in sharing some memories of their dad. I shared my message. It was not anything special but they were gracious to me.

As we sat and ate, one of the sisters told me they would like to get to know Jesus better but did not like coming to church. I suggested that instead of them coming to church why not let us bring church to them. I suggested we plant a cell-group ministry in their home. My pastor helped me explain what a cell ministry was.

The following week we started a new cell ministry in Michelle's home. Many neat things have occurred in this ministry. Within the next four months, Michelle and one of her sisters were baptized and confirmed. Within another month, two of Michelle's nieces and three nephews were baptized.

At the time of writing this chapter, this family is still faithful in their discipleship in spite of some hard times. Since her dad died Michelle's family has gone through a suicide and a house fire, and Michelle is now a single mother and chose to quit school.

They have had more than their share of hardships but they are still hanging in there with Jesus. They were once a family who claimed to hate God and religion. Now they are disciples of Jesus and have discovered their own rich faith lifestyle.

What a difference one little note can make when Jesus uses it.

Final Reflections

- What do you think caused Michelle's family to allow Jesus in their lives? Why do you think hardships still come to their family even after being baptized?
- What is your reflection on this whole experience? How do you see the touch of Jesus in this story?
- Are you familiar with "cell ministry"? What is your opinion of it? How did cell ministry bring a blessing in this situation?
- Tell the group how you found Jesus and how you came in contact with your church.
- If God can use a little note in English class to bring a conversion experience to a family, how much more effective do you think your own testimony of Jesus can be?

What I've Learned

Wow, as I reflect on this experience, there is a bunch of little lessons for me that come to mind. I've learned that God will use the faith of a frightened teenage girl to bring about a great blessing.

I have learned that religious beliefs can bring conflict among family members and that even something as small as a note can be a tool in the hands of Jesus. I learned that follow-up should never wait until tomorrow. We need not put off till tomorrow the things we should be doing today.

I have learned that cell ministry can be a missionary tool to open up families to the joy of the gospel. I have also learned that even when we pray for healing that death can still occur. I learned that a lot of changes can happened in just one weekend.

I also learned to pay better attention to my classmates, because one of them may be the very person God is reaching out to, and God may need me to be bold in my witness with this person. I also learned that God can take even an English class and turn it into something good.

Please be aware of the people around you. Do not take anyone for granted. The people we come in contact with in our everyday walks of life can be the best missionary prospects we have. Pray and ask Jesus to help you have a sensitivity to others. I was almost too preoccupied and self-centered to notice Michelle. If she had not reached out to me, the gospel of Jesus and the ministry of the Community of Christ could never have been offered to her family. Don't get too busy for people.

10
The Miracle of the Prayer Ball

It was a beautiful summer Saturday afternoon. Eight-year-old "Candy Man" was outside playing in the front yard of his grandma's house in an inner-city neighborhood in East Chattanooga. His two brothers and four cousins were also outside enjoying the summer day.

Candy Man was having so much fun playing outside that all his thoughts were good. He was not thinking about his dad, who had died in a car accident two years earlier. He was not thinking about the hard-core lifestyle of his mom, who was doing everything she could to survive the streets, raise three young boys as a single parent, and fight a drug addiction. He also was not thinking about being homeless and being forced to move in with his grandparents again.

All those stressful daily thoughts that often occupied his young mind were nowhere to be found on that warm Saturday afternoon. He was just having fun. Two days before, he turned eight years old. On the very next day, he was going to get to eat a special birthday cake prepared for him personally at the church, the Chattanooga Community of Christ, where his mom had recently been baptized and they all have been attending ever since as a family.

No doubt about it. This sure seemed to be a good day. They had all just eaten ice cream from the local ice cream truck that comes around every weekend. He got crushed candy bar on the top of his chocolate ice cream sundae because he loved candy. What a good day to be a little boy full of life and mischief.

Surely there was nothing that could possibly spoil his day. Not even his two brothers were picking on him. They were being nice to him, maybe because it was his birthday weekend or maybe just because it was a good ole summer day. Everything seemed to be wonderful as young Candy Man walked down the sidewalk.

- What do you remember about spending a day at your grandparents' house as a child? What did you usually do at your grandparents'?
- What is one of the most fun things you did on a warm summer day growing up?
- What is your favorite flavor of ice cream? Did an ice cream truck, with bell ringing, ever come through your neighborhood?
- How do you feel about young Candy Man? Is there any way you relate to him so far in the story?
- Does your church congregation bake birthday cakes for the kids of your group? What special effort does your congregation make to help birthdays be special to your participants?
- What was your family like when you were eight years old? Where did you live? What color was your house? What type of car did you have? How many people were living with you? How much was your family into God at the time?
- Were you attending a church when you were eight years old? Why or why not?

More of the Story:

Suddenly a pickup truck driven by a white man came speeding through the African-American residential neighborhood. The truck jumped the curb and struck little eight-year-old Candy Man. The vehicle dragged him down the sidewalk, back over the curb, and out into the middle of the street where the child was then flipped up into the air, landing on the opposite side of the street.

He had just been standing on the safe sidewalk of his grandma's front yard enjoying a great summer day. Now a truck changed his fun-filled summer day into a nightmare accident which would lead to doctors fighting to save his life.

The driver of the vehicle was drunk and driving the back streets to avoid any contact with police. After striking Candy Man, the driver stopped and got out of his vehicle. He saw the small boy bleeding in the street. He muttered, "Oh, he is OK. God bless this boy. Amen!" He then got back in his vehicle and left the scene.

Rescue workers transported Candy Man to the local children's hospital. His mother called for the pastors of the church to come and join her at the hospital to pray with her and for her son. Doctors told the mother her son had lost a lot of blood and was in critical condition. She was told they first wanted to get him stabilized and make sure he was going to live. If he survived the night, chances were good for survival, but there was also a fear of some brain damage. His injuries included his skull cracked in three places, his jaw and chin broken, cuts in his face requiring several stitches, road burns, bruises, and scratches all over his body as a result of being dragged by the car.

My pastor and I went to the hospital and prayed with the mother. We then went into the ICU to pray with Candy Man. I offered a prayer and my pastor anointed Candy Man's head with oil and then prayed. We also went to pray with the brothers and cousins who had witnessed the whole ordeal. We used the phone and e-mail to gather prayer support from everyone we could.

Not only was Candy Man one of our church participants but he was one of the kids I was assigned to mentor and pastor. Because of my responsibility to mentor him, our relationship was close and my prayers for him were strong.

Reflections

- Have you ever been drunk? Have you ever driven a vehicle after drinking alcohol? How old were you when you took your first drink of alcohol?
- Have you or someone you loved ever been a victim of a drunk driver? Have you ever struck someone while you were driving?
- What do you think about the driver? What do you think about the driver stopping and offering the short prayer?
- What is the worst you have ever been injured?
- When was the last time you visited someone in the hospital and why?
- When was the last time you had your head anointed by a minister and were prayed for?
- What do you think will happen to Candy Man?

More of the Story:

The next day was Sunday and the news was somewhat better. The medical staff felt he was out of any immediate danger of death. They were somewhat amazed at his quick physical recovery.

In addition to the physical injuries, Candy Man was very scared and became withdrawn. Both the doctors and his loved ones were concerned about his emotional and mental healing.

Because of the accident, Candy Man was going to need some surgeries on his face. He was so scared and just lay in the hospital bed looking around. This accident had stolen his energy and playful spirit. His mother was afraid her son would never be the same again.

After Sunday celebration, and the day before his first surgery, our pastor, my mom and dad, and I went to the hospital to see Candy Man again. During the visit, he just lay there and did not respond to anyone.

At church that day I had found a little multicolored bouncing ball outside in the parking lot. I picked it up and put it in my pocket for some reason and forgot about it. As we all stood around the hospital room, I felt the ball in my pocket. I gave it to Candy Man.

I told him the ball was now his. I then offered a prayer for him and prayed that his ball would be used by Jesus to bring healing to my young friend. I prayed that Candy Man would know that his very best friend, Jesus, was holding his hand. I prayed that each time he felt the ball in his hand he would know that Jesus was there on the scene with him, holding his hand.

Reflections

- Candy Man received a broken jaw and chin. What bones have you broken?
- What do you think contributed to his quick physical recovery?
- What is something you have that reminds you that Jesus is with you? What are some common symbols used by Christians to remind us of Jesus?

- Do you remember any story in the Bible where something was blessed and given to people as a reminder of God's love?
- What difference do you think the little ball, given and prayed over by Jared, made?

The Rest of the Story:

After that prayer, Candy Man held onto the ball all night long. The nurse told his mom that Candy Man would not let them take the ball from him so he had it in his hand during the whole surgery and in the recovery room. His jaw was wired shut but he held his ball tight. When he ate or played in the hospital, he put the ball under the blanket right next to him.

He told his mom later, after he went home from the hospital, that the ball was his *prayer ball*. As long as he had that ball he knew Jesus was with him. Candy Man has since returned to his old self. His renewed energy is again getting him into mischief. He recovered rapidly from all his injuries and his fear is gone. Now whenever someone prays at his house, he runs and gets the ball to hold. When someone is sad, Candy Man goes and gets the prayer ball and hands it to them.

He is barely eight years old but already has a testimony of Jesus being with him. He tells everyone — friends, neighbors, classmates, and relatives — that Jesus was with him in the hospital. He then runs and gets his prayer ball and tells them how his pastor blessed the ball to remind him that Jesus was holding his hand.

During our "Yo Buddy" time at church (praising God time), Candy Man often mentions his prayer ball and how he knows that Jesus is holding his hand. After his accident, one of the ministers at church was speaking about the story in the New Testament of Apostle Paul blessing handkerchiefs and giving them to people as a reminder of Jesus. Candy Man immediately began waving his hands and doing everything he could to get the speaker's attention. Finally, he got recognized and blurted out, "God don't use handkerchiefs anymore. Nowaday, his preacher blesses balls. I got one of those prayer balls at my house. Whenever you hold it in your hand, you feel Jesus is with you."

To most people, this incident with the ball may seem silly, but to us the prayer ball is a symbol and a reminder of Jesus' promise that he will be with us always. Jesus is with us even when a fun summer day is turned into a nightmare by a drunk driver.

I don't think Candy Man or his family will ever forget that Jesus is holding their hands. They have become a very faithful family at church. Candy Man has become an inviter. At the time of writing this chapter, I can think of about eleven new people we now have as participants because of his invitation.

Candy Man's family has a new home just a few houses down from his grandparents. His mom has a new job and is able to pay her own bills. She has started back to church and is getting help for her addictions. The drunk driver was arrested about a week after the hit-and-run accident. His trial has not yet come up.

Just the other day at church, Candy Man's mom did the "Getting Real with Jesus Time" portion of the celebration worship. Her testimony was that since the prayer ball incident, her family life has changed so much. She said God is always on their hearts. She even offered a prayer that the drunk driver who hit her son could find "the real Jesus" and peace in his life. She said the prayer ball reminds her whole family that Jesus is holding our hands on our good days and especially on our bad days.

Final Reflections

- What do think about the prayer ball? Why do you think it brought so much hope to Candy Man and his mom?

- How do you feel about his mom praying for the drunk driver?
- How easy is it for you to remember that Jesus is with us always, especially on bad days?
- What are you personally doing to help keep drunk drivers off the road?
- Please pray for Candy Man's family to stay healthy and close to God.

What I've Learned

In the world we live in, our lives can go from fun and peaceful to dangerous and painful in the blink of an eye. This is why we must be sure we take Jesus with us daily and never take life or our loved ones for granted.

The awesome power of Jesus can use even a small, multicolored rubber ball to bring about the miracle of hope. I've learned that taking chances in a vehicle is selfish and dangerous. Driving is risky enough without adding drugs and alcohol to the situation.

I learned that an innocent little boy can be hurt standing on the sidewalk, and there is no reason for it. It is just life. Life is full of good days and bad days regardless of our efforts. I know a severely injured boy can put his faith in Jesus and prayer and sometimes receive a mighty miracle.

I know that if my young friend, Candy Man, can find the courage and faith to invite others to come to Jesus, there is really no excuse for any of us not to be bold in our inviting spirit.

11
Fear in the House

Have you ever been so afraid that the palms of your hands were sweating and you could hear the beating of your own heart? Unfortunately I have encountered this type of fear several times already in my life. Usually the fear is not about what might happen to me. Instead it is a concern for others and my own insecurity that I may be helpless in sparing someone else from further pain or harm.

This chapter is about one of those experiences, which occurred just a few weeks ago in my own driveway. Since moving to Chattanooga to plant a church ministry focusing on hard-living and hardcore people in society, we have lived in the same house in the same neighborhood. From our first day here we have reached out to our neighbors and have seen many of them respond to our invitations.

Folks from our home neighborhood have attended many activities in our house: Kids Bible Club, teenage WWJD Club, family cell groups, teen cell groups, Sunday school classes, and worship celebrations. Our home has been the location for baby blessings, baptisms, confirmations, evangelist blessings, weddings, administrations to the sick, a couple of funeral memorials, and even one ordination service.

Our home has hosted neighborhood watch meetings, Christmas parties, wedding showers, home improvement meetings, and countless overnight safe parties for kids or teenagers. The truth is, probably someone from every house in our subdivision has been in our home at one time or another. Everyone knows we are a ministry family. This has proved to be both a blessing and a curse.

Many times when our neighbors have been in trouble due to abuse, domestic violence, crime, and other crises, they have pounded on our door or run into our garage where my dad's office is located, seeking safety and help. This is the hard thing about having an open home. Any time of day or night, no matter what special event or normal family activity is occurring, your life will be interrupted and your plans will change. Privacy and "time off" is not a normal thing in the life of a front-line missionary.

Most of the time when this happens it is my dad or mom who has to respond to the crisis and new opportunity for ministry. But not this time—it was my turn to react to a plea for help.

Reflections

- Can you think of the time in your life when you were most afraid?
- How many of your neighbors do you know personally? Have you been inside many of your neighbors' homes? How often does a neighbor come to your house?
- Do you feel you have made a positive difference in your neighborhood? What ways have you helped your neighborhood be a better place to live?
- What was the last worship experience in your home?
- Have you ever invited a neighbor to a worship experience? What happened?
- Has one of your neighbors ever come to your house seeking safety or assistance? What happened?

More of the Story:

My mom had hurt her back and was unable to get out of bed very easily or go to work. Therefore, Dad stuck close to the house for a few days to offer her whatever she needed. When I got home from school, I stayed home while Dad left to take care of ministry.

Mom had fallen asleep in her bed so I decided to go outside and get in some basketball practice. I moved the cars around in our driveway to give me room to run and dribble. I had just worked up a good sweat and begun shooting some baskets. I have been coached not to shoot around until I have gotten a little tired because if you can jump and make baskets when you are tired, you definitely can make them when you are at full energy. Therefore, I had just pushed myself physically enough to be feeling a little tired.

I had really just started shooting around when a little neighborhood boy ran up to me screaming, "A man is trying to kill my mom and sisters. You got to come and help me. Please help me. Please help me." I had never seen this little boy before in my neighborhood but without thinking I grabbed his hand and ran with him to a house down the road.

When I got to his house, fear grabbed me. Maybe it was because I remembered that the neighbor who lives at that address is a big guy who works as a bouncer. Or maybe I was afraid that I would make the whole situation worse. Whatever the reason, I was scared—so scared that the only thing I knew to do was pray. I prayed out loud asking God to give me courage and wisdom and to send my dad home fast.

I asked God to send me some help, even if it was a cop. No sooner than my prayer ended, my fear was gone. It really was a strange experience. Just a few seconds earlier I was frozen with fear and could hear my heartbeat. But now, after pausing to pray, there was no fear in me. I had peace, and it was just so obvious to me that it was the prayer that replaced my fear with that peace.

The voice of the little boy broke into my reflections: "My little brother and sisters are in there. They might be dead. Please help them."

Reflections

- Have you ever found peace and courage through prayer?
- Do you know anyone who is or has been a bouncer?

- What do you think the danger was inside the neighbor's house?
- How do you think you would handle the situation if you were in Jared's shoes?
- How do you feel about the little boy and his desperate plea for help?

The Rest of the Story:

I don't know what I was thinking, or maybe I wasn't thinking at all. I ran into this house full of apparent strangers with no idea what I was going to find inside. I couldn't wait any longer. There was something wrong inside the house. I couldn't run back to my house because in a crisis every second is crucial. I took a deep breath and ran into the house knowing that Jesus was going to be with me.

When I got inside I saw three small children hiding under a table. It was easy to sense their fear. I knelt down by them and put my finger to my lips, signaling to them to be quiet. The smallest one grabbed my neck and held me tight. I told them to run outside to their brother. They did not say a word. They just ran as fast as they could.

As I knelt on my knees under the table that had been the kids' hiding place, I tried to collect my thoughts on what to do next. I heard the door behind me close and whipped my head around to see who it was. To my great delight, it was my dad. When I saw him standing there, I whispered to myself, "Thank you, God. You are so awesome!"

Together we started to walk quietly through the house. Dad explained to me later that he had felt a need to come home for some reason. He said that as he topped the hill to our house, he saw me running with the little boy down the street. He parked his car in our driveway and followed after me.

As we walked through the house, we finally saw a woman hiding behind a big chair and holding her face in her hands. She had been beaten up and blood was running down her face. We helped her outside, where her children met her. They hugged and wept.

Almost as soon as we walked outside, a police car pulled up. We flagged it down and told the officer we needed help. He said he was looking for a dog, and his search had brought him to our neighborhood. To me, it was no dog that brought the cop. It was the grace of God in response to the prayer of this fear-frozen teenage minister that brought the police officer here.

He talked to the woman, and within minutes more police arrived. They went into the house and came out with a man in handcuffs. The man was not the bouncer we knew. They put him into the police car and an ambulance came for the woman. The police took statements from Dad and me, then sent us home.

We have not seen anyone at the house since. I have no idea what happened. I don't know if the man was arrested or how bad the woman was hurt. I don't know where the boy is who came and got me. I know they are safe because the police took care of the situation. But the house remains empty even as I write this.

There have been several rumors in the neighborhood about the situation, but no real facts. Our inquiries with police have not gained us any information. We just hope and pray that this family will allow God to bless them.

Final Reflections

- What are your reflections on this experience? Do you think Jared was just lucky or do you think maybe some special help came his way?
- Why do you think Jared's dad felt the need to come home? Have you ever felt the need to do something? If so, what did you do with that feeling?
- Have you ever been a victim of domestic violence? What can we do as Christians to help cut down on domestic violence?
- Pray now for God to grant us wisdom and courage to know how we can put an end to domestic violence in our neighborhoods.

What I've Learned

For my parents, this isn't anything new. They've been involved in several similar situations and just take it in stride. For me, I don't like these types of surprises and hope that I never again have to be in such a situation.

However, my testimony is this: God sure does answer prayer. I was so nervous, but after praying I just knew things would be all right. I prayed for Dad to come home and there he was. Cops *never* come through our neighborhood and yet there was one driving by right when we needed him. I know prayer doesn't always work this way and things don't normally fall into place. But I sure am glad that the mysterious workings of God came to the rescue this time.

I don't know why family violence seems to be growing. I don't know why the little boy ran to me, why I was so afraid, or why my prayer was answered so quickly. I don't know why sometimes things seem to work out when we exercise our faith in prayer and sometimes things seem to just get worse. I just know that *this* time I asked and I received.

In this situation I had plenty of fear. I could almost taste it. Yet my fear wasn't strong enough to keep the power of prayer from rescuing the day. I am a personal witness that your faith can give you greater strength than your fear. Fear can cause you to run faster than ever or to fight back stronger than normal. But faith in Jesus and the power of prayer can cause you to stand firm, face dangers you are not capable of handling on your own, and rise above your fear to do what must be done.

This time God answered my prayer. Well, I am just a teenager and I know I have much to learn. I sure cannot explain how prayer works and I don't even feel I need to try. But I do know that faith in God and in the power of prayer is much stronger than our fears. Please don't stop believing in prayer. Don't let your fears cause you to hide your faith in God. Always be found having enough faith and courage to get involved when help is needed. Your faith is making a difference. Keep praying. Keep being generous. Keep standing strong and brave, because you and I know faith is much more powerful than fear. Please pray that someday, as disciples of Jesus, we can find a cure for domestic violence and abuse.

12
Maggie at the Midnight Movies

One of my Dad-and-son traditions is going to midnight movies on the weekend. Midnight movies are seldom crowded and often empty. It is neat and fun to be in a big theater with just my dad and maybe a couple of my friends. Our lives are always active and full. My parents are very open and generous with their life together. Seldom has there been a time when just my parents and I were alone.

My dad is a cool, funny, and full-of-life kind of guy. He is definitely a big kid at heart when the burdens of ministry are not weighing him down. Make no mistake about it—when you minister to hard-living and hard-core people in nearly hopeless situations in this great country of ours, a minister's heart is very heavy at times. There are no books that can prepare him or her for the loneliness and the price of discipleship that is required. True disciple-makers will seldom share their full pain of the high price of ministry with you because, unless you have paid it yourself, there is no way you can possibly understand it. Trust me on this one.

Therefore the midnight movies are a special treat for me to be just with Dad. We usually eat hot wings or pizza and then go to a movie. We watch all types of movies. Dad is his silly and outrageous true self and keeps my friends and me laughing and longing for more of his precious time. I do not think I will ever forget my movie times with my dad. Many times before or after the movie, he and I share in some serious conversations.

I enjoy the food and the movies on our late nights out. But my favorite time is our discussions after the movies. It is personal bonding time when I get to see a side of my dad that very few people are privileged to see. These are times when Dad shares his personal dreams, disappointments, hopes, fears, and other stuff like that.

It is Dad's personal sharing that causes him to be one of my greatest heroes. Believe me, I am well aware of his humanness and we clash often. But my entire life I have witnessed his courage in being generous with his heart. I know that many times his big heart has been broken by so many he loves. Not so much broken by any of our family members, but broken through his efforts at being a bold witness of Jesus and so generous with his hope and strong belief in the real, life-changing gospel.

This chapter is about one of those midnight movie experiences. I think I learned one or two of those hidden mysteries of the kingdom that I hear church people talk about sometimes.

Reflections

- What is one thing you used to do with your dad or mom that is a fond memory for you?
- What is your favorite kind of movie? What was the last movie you saw in a theater?
- Who are two of your personal heroes and why?
- The author speaks of the "courage to be generous." What do you think that means?
- What do you think or feel about the author's following statement: "True disciple-makers will seldom share their full pain of the high price of ministry with you because, unless you have paid it yourself, there is no way you can possibly understand it. Trust me on this one."
- Do you think it takes a different kind of discipleship to minister to hard-core people than other types of people? Why or why not?

More of the Story:

Dad and I had just gotten out of a late-night movie and decided to stop by an all-night hamburger place to get a Cherry Vanilla Coke. While we sat there, Dad got very quiet and his thoughts drifted away from our setting.

I just sat there awhile. Finally I broke the silence by asking what he was thinking about. He apologized and said he was worrying about Maggie.

Maggie had been gone from Chattanooga for several months so I was surprised at Dad for thinking about her. I asked him if he had heard from her lately. He said not really, just through a few e-mails and everything seemed fine. But he still insisted that she was in some kind of trouble.

We then changed the subject and enjoyed our cheeseburgers and Cherry Vanilla Cokes. We talked about the movie. Dad told some of his funny stories. I caught him up on the happenings of my young life. We got back in the car and headed home.

While we were driving I told Dad that I had noticed throughout my life that my parents had kind of a sixth sense about people we knew. I have grown to know that when someone comes to my parents' minds that they were usually right on.

I could never remember having that sixth-sense type of thing. I asked Dad how he developed such a skill. He first told me that it was not a sixth sense, supernatural, or magical. He said it was just the power of love, compassion, and prayer.

He said that when you allow yourself to become close to people through genuine caring and you have a pretty strong prayer life, where you work to keep a good relationship with Jesus alive, sometimes you just feel or know things. Dad said it was hard to explain, but that he tried to pay attention to his thoughts and feelings because once in a while it is the Holy Spirit leading. He said everyone has those types of thoughts and feelings, but most people just ignore them. My mom had taught him through their many years of marriage to be sensitive to his inner feelings and thoughts.

As we continued to travel, I sought to comfort my dad from his worries about Maggie. I mentioned all the good changes I had seen in Maggie's life. She had been baptized, quit smoking, stopped stripping, and was now teaching Sunday school and serving as a Bible school director.

He said those changes were all great blessings and miracles. But he said she was still using Jesus to try to escape from her past and her sins. He said many Christians try to use Jesus to escape from life's pain instead of allowing Jesus to set them free. He said there is a big difference between escaping prison or captivity and being set free from it.

He told me that part of Jesus' mission as Savior of the world is to set the captives free but most folks hope Jesus will just help them escape. Escaping is temporary; being set free is forever. He said he wished he were a better minister and mentor because he had failed so many times in helping people discover the "setting-free" ministry of Jesus.

Dad explained that he was afraid that many times people like Maggie do good and religious things in an attempt to escape from past pain. Once we are set free from our pain and failures, that becomes the greatest tool for witnessing we have to offer Jesus. But when we try to escape, our past and failures often catch up with and destroy us.

I must admit, I am still not sure what all this means but I do know there is a deep truth that was shared with me on that midnight-movie night. His fear for Maggie had something to do with his belief that she was trying to escape instead of allowing Jesus to teach her the hard work that leads to getting set free.

I need to catch you up on Maggie.

Reflections

- If you wanted a late-night snack, what would it probably be and where would you probably get it? Have you ever had a Cherry Vanilla Coke? What is your favorite soft drink?
- Can you remember any bits of wisdom that your parents or grandparents ever shared with you?

- Have you or anyone you know ever had kind of a sixth sense about people or events? What is your view of Jared's dad's explanation of such things?
- What do you think Jared's dad meant by there being a difference between escaping and being set free? Do you agree or disagree with the statement that many Christians seek escape from pain instead of seeking the setting-free ministry of Jesus?
- So far in this experience, what do you know about Maggie?

More of the Story:

I first met Maggie when I was probably eight or nine. You know, the age where boys start liking girls but won't admit it. I thought Maggie was a real fox. You know, very attractive. Whenever she spoke to me, I would get all tongue-tied. She was probably ten or twelve years older than me but I think I had a little boy's crush on her.

My family met her through another former stripper whom my family had helped to discover Jesus and a new, safer lifestyle. She later died of AIDS, but before her death she helped our church reach out to other strippers and was fairly successful in helping many find better lifestyles. Maggie was one of those women.

Maggie's parents were very active in the "swinger lifestyle" and therefore it was easy for Maggie to fall into an active sex life at an early age. She had two abortions before we even met her.

But through the cell ministry of our church, Maggie found the courage to walk away from the adult industry. She went to a rehab program and got off drugs. She was buried in a mountain of debt before she was even nineteen years old, but through the help of several programs she was able to get that taken care of, too.

She was baptized and became an active member in the Community of Christ. Maggie seemed to get involved in every good program and organization she could get involved with. It was as if she was trying to make up for years of being selfish.

She lived with us for a little while, and she and my mom became close. She got a job and her own apartment; then she met a man at work and they got married. Mom and Dad performed the wedding ceremony, which was held in our house.

Shortly after the wedding they moved about a hundred miles outside Chattanooga. There were no Community of Christ congregations in their new community but they traveled to Chattanooga every now and then for worship. Eventually, they got involved in another church near their home. Maggie got very involved in her new church as a Sunday school teacher and choir member, and was doing church things daily.

We were all proud of her because she was doing so well in her new life. However, Dad did not always show great joy about her accomplishments. I remember him telling Mom and me that he felt guilty about not feeling good about her. He said he didn't think it was because she changed churches because he knew her new church was closer, larger, more traditional, safer, and had more to offer in many ways. He said maybe he was just jealous of the other church or something. One of my dad's faults is he always blames himself for bad feelings he has instead of accepting them as insights.

Over the years our contact with Maggie decreased but was still steady. I must admit, with the new contacts we get each week and with all our participants, Miss Maggie did not come to my mind very often. Therefore, I was somewhat surprised when her name came up as the reason for the interruption of our late-night movie night.

Reflections

- Who was the older woman or man you can first remember having a crush on?
- The author speaks about Maggie's parents being involved in a "swinger lifestyle." Have you ever heard of that lifestyle before?
- Maggie used to drive more than a hundred miles to attend church. What is the longest distance you ever travel to be part of a congregation?
- What is your reaction to Maggie so far in the story? What is your reaction to Jared's dad's concern for her in light of all the positive lifestyle changes she was making?

More of the Story:

When Dad and I got home from our movie night I suggested that we pray for Maggie. He agreed. We stood in our family room and offered prayers for her. I noticed during our prayers that Dad was shedding tears. After the prayer, I hugged my dad and told him to remember that Jesus was on the scene.

The next day was Sunday and so we went to church. We did our normal Sunday thing with worship celebrations, our neighborhood lunch, bible studies and open center time. We then helped transport kids home from church and went to our leadership team meeting.

We had left home around 8:30 a.m. and returned around 11 p.m. It was pretty much a typical Sunday for us except for one thing: There were about eleven voice messages on our home phone. Most people who know us usually call our cell phones, not our home phone.

As my mom checked the messages, she told me to run downstairs to get Dad. He was taking the trash out, which was normally my job. Dad usually just did stuff like trash collecting and dishes if there was something heavy on his mind. So when I saw him hauling trash to the curb, I asked him what was up. He laughed and said, "I just can't shake Maggie being on my mind. I am going to go e-mail her."

I told him that Mom wanted to talk to him upstairs. With that, he gave me back the trash pickup job and told me to be sure to feed our dogs. As Dad headed upstairs to talk to Mom, all I could think was, Dang, how come I get stuck doing so much *work*?

When I came back upstairs, Dad was on the phone. Mom told me that Maggie on the previous night, our movie night, had killed herself by using her car's exhaust fumes. Dad was being asked to share in the funeral service. Wow, I just sat down, thinking about Maggie and feeling compassion for my dad.

I thought about how awful it must be to be him right then. He had sensed something was wrong with her and that she was in danger. He felt helpless in not knowing what to do, and now she was dead. Yes, I know it was hell for her family but I knew my dad was also carrying a little bit of hell in his own heart right then.

Maggie had begun drinking and getting high again during the previous few months and hiding her return to these addictions by her many activities. Her husband had recently found out about her return to an addictive lifestyle and confronted her a few days earlier.

It was decided that Dad and Maggie's new minister would share together in the memorial service responsibilities. My mom was asked to join five other women as the pallbearers. I thought that was kind of a different thing because normally I only saw men carry caskets, not six women.

Reflections

- What is a normal Sunday schedule for you and your family? What time do you leave for church? get home from church?
- Whose job is it at home to take out the trash?

- How do you feel about Maggie? Do you think she will go to hell for her act of suicide? In what ways do you think she was hiding her addictive return? Do you feel most people have things they are trying to hide?
- Jared mentioned that he felt his dad was experiencing a "little bit of hell." Do you agree or disagree with this?
- Have you ever seen six women serve as pallbearers for a funeral? Have you ever been a pallbearer?

The Rest of the Story:

The memorial service ended up with just Dad doing it. Maggie's new minister told her family that she would burn in hell for her acts of abortions and suicide. I sat there in the room with my dad when the other minister was telling the family these things.

The family members began to cry. A debate broke out among some family members over the issue of the consequences of suicide. The other minister told the family he was sorry but *he* was not judging Maggie; the *scriptures* were judging her.

Well, at this point my Dad sprang into action. His actions will not be written about here. All I will say is when Dad finally took action, everybody was paying attention. Dad's view was completely different from the other minister.

After the conflict ended, the family unanimously agreed that it would be best for Dad to do the memorial service. I know he felt terrible about the whole incident, but he was not going to allow this family to be abused in their greatest moment of sorrow and need.

However, Dad would not end up doing the service alone. I was drafted into sharing the responsibilities. Dad did an awesome job at the service. He quoted a song about a person dying and standing at the gates of heaven. The keeper of the gates was turning the person away from heaven when a voice was heard. The voice said, "This one's with me." It was the voice of Jesus.

Dad made it clear to everyone that he believed Maggie was with Jesus, not in hell. He talked about the grace of God and how the love of Jesus would cause our Master to say to any doubters about Maggie's place in eternity that "This one's with me." He said he felt that Jesus was welcoming Maggie into his house of many mansions because our Father in heaven had a big, big house with lots of rooms.

Well, Dad got some people almost cheering his words and yet others were wanting to stone him because he was speaking against the so-called "teaching of scripture." I am just a teenager and I do not know much. I don't know if my dad's views about Maggie's place in eternal life are wrong or right. But I will tell you that Maggie's family gained great comfort from his words. I felt Jesus' arms around me during that time. I also want you to know that within the next three months following her death, three of Maggie's relatives and four of her friends were baptized. To my knowledge they are all still serving Jesus and living out their commitments in their lifestyles.

Again, in my young life I personally saw Jesus take a horrible and deeply sad situation and use it to bring about a positive witness of the grace of God and the unconditional love of his kingdom.

Final Reflections

- What is your reaction to this experience? to the other minister's words? to Jared's dad's response?
- If you had been at this service, would you have been upset or encouraged by the words Jared described?
- What is the most disturbing part of this experience to you? What is the most inspiring part?

- Why do you think some of Maggie's relatives and friends were baptized within weeks of this experience?
- In what ways have you personally experienced the grace of God in your life?

What I've Learned

Wow, I am still learning from this experience. Even as I write this on paper, I reflect back to the lessons I learned. I have learned that we need to discover the "setting the captive free" ministry of Jesus Christ and not get caught up in our attempts to escape or hide in our busy acts of service.

My dear sister Maggie was not only the older woman of my first childhood crush but the first person to teach me about the need for the setting-free ministry of the gospel. I have learned that we need to be more sensitive to the promptings of the Holy Spirit that often come through our own thoughts and feelings.

I learned about the grace of God and the true salvation of Jesus that extend even beyond our current life. I learned that well-intended people, even ministers, can bring further pain and hopelessness into people's lives when they use the scriptures as a weapon of judgment instead of an instrument of peace, hope, invitation, and witness.

I learned that my dad, with all his doubts and faults, is a proclaimer of the gospel even when it is unpopular. I hope I can find the same courage to stand against the abuses that all too often take place in the name of Jesus.

I learned that keeping your relationship alive with Jesus takes courage and a daily focus. I learned that I am very blessed to have been raised in a home where grace abounds.